ENGLISH READING

FOR COLLEGE STUDENTS

Edited with Notes
By Byung-Seok Oh

Shinasa

C·O·N·T·E·N·T·S

1

WHAT TO DO WITH YOUR COLLEGE LIFE

by Roger W. Holmes

Why are you going to college? Not to enhance your parents' social position; not to get high marks; not to get the ultimate answers, which not even we can furnish. To use our own professional jargon, you come to college to get a liberal education[1]. We must admit that we do not altogether know what a liberal education is, but we have some fairly good ideas on the subject. We do not entirely follow these ideas. None of us, for example, believes that there is a magic in piling up a certain number of hour-credits. Yet, sixty credits and you will get your diploma. And that diploma is supposed to admit you to the company of educated men and women. Why not fifty-five, or sixty-five? We do not know. Indeed if you pressed us we should have to admit that some students are liberally educated with thirty credits while others will not belong to the educated company if they take sixty times sixty hours of credit. Do not measure your education by simple arithmetic.

Do not select your courses with an eye to[2] a specific job or type of occupation. More of you will make this mistake than not, and it is one of the most serious you can make. In the first place, we know at least that a liberal education involves a balance and harmony of interests. Secondly, your interests and talents are by no means fully appreciated or explored when you come to

1. liberal education: 일반교양교육(직업, 전문교육에 대하여 인격, 교양 교육을 주로 한다).
2. with an eye to: ~을 목적으로 하여

us. You do not want to wake up in your senior year and wish that you had not missed many important and interesting things. Thousands of seniors do.

When you come to college you are intellectually very young and have not yet learned to proceed safely or efficiently under your own intellectual power. You are what your environment and your elders have made you. Your ideas are not your own. The first thing you must learn is to stand on your own ideas. This is why you should not take us and our ideas too seriously. Broaden your horizon so that as you become more and more able to take care of yourself you will move intelligently. Do considerable mental visiting in your first years in college. Try encounter the major points of view represented on the faculty and among the students. Entertain[1] them the more seriously the more they differ from your own. You may return to your own, but if you do it will be with greater tolerance and broader understanding.

You come to college to gain a liberal perspective. In gaining this perspective you must come to know the nature which surrounds and compels you, the society with which you must live and cooperate, the creative spirit which is your heritage, and the tools of language and of thought. To express it in this specific manner is helpful. It suggests certain intellectual virtues which you must possess before you can be considered an educated man or woman.

For example, we have said that you must come to know the natural world. This does not mean that you must study physics and chemistry and astronomy and geology. It means that you must acquire the scientific attitude, understand the atmosphere and significance of the exact sciences, know their fundamental assumptions, their key concepts, their major contributions. And the same is true of the biological sciences. A course in botany and zoology or physiology or psychology is enough to give you an understanding of the important aspects of biology. You have not time for them all. But one is essential. Far too many are ignorant of the biological forces affecting human conduct. You should get into the laboratory while you are in college, and you should work in both the exact and the biological sciences.

---

1. entertain: to allow oneself to think about; have in mind; consider

You want also to[1] know the society with which you must live and cooperate. And one of the way in which you want to know it is the historical. You must be historically minded. You must recognize the importance of the past for the present. Man learns by experience, and history is social experience. Greek, Roman, European, Asian history—you cannot study them all, but you can become historically minded. And you can become socially minded in your view of the present world. Economic, social and political forces have your world in their grips. You must study these forces, measure them, evaluate them.

Our heritage in the field of the arts has always been recognized as liberalizing. Not so much need to urge you here. Most of the greatest interpretation of human living is to be found in painting, sculpture, music and literature. What are some of the things which the great creative geniuses have told us about ourselves? What are modern artists trying to do? You must find out these things, not just that you may go to museums and concerts, but that you may want to go to museums and concerts. Elect some art or music, for pleasure, but also to increase your knowledge. Also, get a full and enthusiastic knowledge of the literature of your mother tongue. You will have discovered a source of wisdom, good taste and pleasure. Such studies need no recommendation.

Finally, you must come to understand the tools of language and of thought. And here urging is necessary. You ought to know another language, ancient or modern, inflected or noninflected, so well that you dream in it. Such knowledge gives a far better understanding of your own tongue, both as a tool and as an art, than you could otherwise obtain. And you will have another literature open to you. Futhermore, you should conversant[2] with the structures and powers of thought as an intellectual tool, and you should be willing to examine fundamental assumptions. Mathematics, logic and philosophy are helpful here. You may think them difficult, do not avoid them altogether.

If you will examine this program[3] for the enlarging of your

1. want: 다음에 to부정사를 동반하여 "~해야 한다"(should)로 쓰임.
2. conversant: familiar or acquainted(with), esp. as a result of study or experience
3. program: a prospectus or syllabus, curriculum

intellectual horizon you will see that it involves some eight subjects spread throughout the departments of your college. It is a program which you can complete in your freshman and sophomore years and one which you should carry through[1] in order that you may be equipped intellectually to proceed to the second part of your college education. It will give you necessary breadth.

But you must also specialize, when the foundation has been laid. You must do this not because specialization will prepare you for a specific job, but because a certain degree of specialization is the second essential of true intellectual endeavor. Without specialization your college work is in danger of becoming that thin veneer[2] of "culture" which we all recognize as superficial. And now you will find the faculty more cooperative. We are specialists and we like to encourage specialization. But still be on your guard[3], for we shall mislead you by overemphasizing the importance of our particular little corners of learning. The important matter is not what you specialize in, but that you specialize. Specialization for its own sake, that is my point.

You should devote half of your last two years to intensive specialization in one subject in which you have the greatest interest and for which you have shown marked talent. Perhaps you have found history the most absorbing of subjects. Good! Go on in it. Devote half of your junior and senior years to history. Show that you can work intensively on the details of your chosen major, manipulate[4] these details correctly, and fit them into a comprehensive picture of the whole. But remember—though your teachers will work against you here—remembering that you are studying primarily for the sake of the intensive specialization and not of the history. Your roommate is getting specialization and not of the history. Your roommate is getting the same thing from majoring in mathematics or English literature.

When you have avoided the Scylla[5] of heterogeneous

1. carry through: ~을 완성하다, 성취하다
2. veneer: any attractive but superficial appearance or display, 겉치장, 허식
3. on one's guard: 조심하여, 경계하여
4. manipulate: to work, operate, or treat with or as with the hand or hands; handle or use, esp. with skill
5. Scylla: a dangerous rock on the Italian side of the Straits of Messina, opposite

meanderings among elementary facts and concepts and the Charybdis[1] of a study so narrow that you are ignorant of what is going on outside your own little corner of interest, you will have intellectual balance and perspective.

the whirlpool Charybdis: in classical mythology both Scylla and Charybdis were personified as female monsters

1. Charybdis: old name of a whirlpool off the NE coast of Sicily, in the Strait of Messina(now called Galofalo)

AFTER YOU READ

1. According to the author, why are you going to college?

2. What is the first thing you must learn?

3. In gaining a liberal perspective, what must you come to know?

4. If you know another language, what can such knowledge give you?

5.. In order that you may be equipped intellectually to proceed to the second part of your college education, what should you carry through?

6. Without specialization what would your college work become?

7. To have intellectual balance and perspective, what should you do?

2

OPRAH WINFREY: STANFORD UNIVERSITY COMMENCEMENT SPEECH 2008

by Oprah Winfrey

Thank you, President Hennessy, and to the trustees and the faculty, to all of the parents and grandparents, to you, the Stanford graduates. Thank you for letting me share this amazing day with you.

I need to begin by letting everyone in on a little secret. The secret is that Kirby Bumpus, Stanford Class of '08, is my goddaughter. So, I was thrilled when President Hennessy asked me to be your Commencement speaker, because this is the first time I've been allowed on campus since Kirby's been here.

You see, Kirby's a very smart girl. She wants people to get to know her on her own terms, she says. Not in terms of who she knows. So, she never wants anyone who's first meeting her to know that I know her and she knows me. So, when she first came to Stanford for new student orientation with her mom, I hear that they arrived and everybody was so welcoming, and somebody came up to Kirby and they said, "Ohmigod, that's Gayle King!" Because a lot of people know Gayle King as my BFF [Best Friend Forever].

And so somebody comes up to Kirby, and they say, "Ohmigod, is that Gayle King?" And Kirby's like, "h-huh. She's my mom."

And so the person says, Ohmigod, does it mean, like, you

know Oprah Winfrey?"

And Kirby says, "Sort of."

I said, "Sort of? You sort of know me?" Well, I have photographic proof. I have pictures which I can e-mail to you all of Kirby riding horsey with me on all fours[1]. So, I more than sort-of know Kirby Bumpus. And I'm so happy to be here, just happy that I finally, after four years, get to see her room. There's really nowhere else I'd rather be, because I'm so proud of kirby, who graduates today with two degrees, one in human bio and the other in psychology. Love you, Kirby Cakes! That's how well I know her. I can call her Cakes.

And so proud of her mother and father, who helped her get through this time, and her brother, Will. I really had nothing to do with her graduating from Stanford, but every time anybody's asked me in the past couple of weeks what I was doing, I would say, "I'm getting ready to go to Stanford"

I just love saying "Stanford." Because the truth is, I know I would have never gotten my degree at all, 'cause I didn't go to Stanford. I went to Tennessee State University. But I never would have gotten my diploma at all, because I was supposed to graduate back in 1975, but I was short one credit. And I figured, I'm just going to forget it, 'cause, you know, I'm not going to march with my class. Because by that point, I was already on television. I'd been in television since I was 19 and a sophomore. Granted, I was the only television anchor person that had an 11 0'clock curfew doing the 10 0'clock news.

Seriously, my dad was like, "Well, that news is over at 10:30. Be home by 11."

But that didn't matter to me, because I was earning a living. I was on my way. So, I thought, I'm going to let this college thing

1. If you are on all fours, your knees, feet, and hands are on the ground. • She crawled on all fours over to the window.

go and I only had one credit short. But, my father, from that time on and for years after, was always on my case[1], because I did not graduate. He'd say, "Oprah Gail"—that's my middle name -" I don't know what you're gonna do without that degree." And I'd say, "But, Dad, I have my own television show."

And he'd say, "Well, I still don't know what you're going to do without that degree."

And I'd say, "But, Dad, now I'm a talk show host." He'd say, "I don't know how you're going to get another job without that degree."

So, in 1987, Tennessee State University invited me back to speak at their commencement. By then, I had my own show, was nationally syndicated[2]. I'd made a movie, had been nominated for an Oscar and founded my company, Harpo. But I told them, I cannot come and give a speech unless I can earn one more credit, because my dad's still saying I'm not going to get anywhere without that degree

So, I finished my coursework, I turned in my final paper and I got the degree.

And my dad was very proud. And I know that, if anything happens, that one credit will be my salvation.

But I also know why my dad was insisting on that diploma, because, as B. B. King put it, "The beautiful thing about learning is that nobody can take that away from you." And learning is really in the broadest sense what I want to talk about today, because your education, of course, isn't ending here. In many ways, it only just begun.

The world has so many lessons to teach you. I consider the

1. If you say that someone is on the case, you mean that they are aware of a particular problem and are trying to resolve it.
2. When newspaper articles or television programs are syndicated, they are sold to several different newspaper or television stations, who then publish the articles or broadcast the programmes. • Today his programm is syndicated to 500 stations.

world, this Earth, to be like a school and our life the classrooms. And sometimes here in this Planet Earth school the lessons often come dressed up as detours or roadblocks. And sometimes as full-blown crises. And the secret I've learned to getting ahead[1] is being open to the lessons, lessons from the grandest university of all, that is, the universe itself.

It's being able to walk through life eager and open to self-improvement and that which is going to best help you evolve, 'cause that's really why we're here, to evolve as human beings. To grow into[2] more of ourselves, always moving to the next level of understanding, the next level of compassion and growth.

I think about one of the greatest compliment I've ever received: I interviewed with a reporter when I was first starting out in Chicago. And then many years later, I saw the same reporter. And she said to me, "You know what? You really haven't changed. You've just become more of yourself."

And that is really what we're all trying to do, become more of ourselves. And I believe that there's a lesson in almost everything that you do and every experience, and getting the lesson is how you move forward. It's how you enrich your spirit. And, trust me, I know that inner wisdom is more precious than wealth. The more you spend it, the more you gain.

So, today, I just want to share a few lessons—meaning three—that I've learned in my journey so far. And aren't you glad? Don't you hate it when somebody says, "I'm going to share a few," and it's 10 lessons later? And, you're like, "Listen, this is my graduation. This is not about you." So, it's only going to be three.

The three lessons that have had the greatest impact on my life have to do with feelings, with failure and with finding happiness.

---

1. If you want to get ahead, you want to be successful in your career. • He wanted safety, security, a home, and a chance to get ahead.(=get on)
2. When a child grows into an item of clothing, they become taller or bigger so that it fits them properly. • It's a bit big, but she'll soon grow into it.

A year after I left college, I was given the opportunity to co-anchor the 6 o'clock news in Baltimore, because the whole goal in the media at the time I was coming up was you try to move to larger markets. And Baltimore was a much larger market than Nashville. So, getting the 6 o'clock news co-anchor job at 22 was such a big deal. It felt like the biggest deal in the world at the time.

And I was so proud, because I was finally going to have my chance to be like Barbara Walters, which is who I had been trying to emulate since the start of my TV career. So I was 22 years old, making $22,000 a year. And it's where I met my best friend, Gayle, who was an intern at the same TV station. And once we become friends, we'd say, "Ohmigod, I can't believe it! You're making $22,000 and you're only 22. Imagine when you're 40 and you're making $40,000!"

When I turned 40, I was so glad that didn't happen.

So, here I am, 22, making $22,000 a year and, yet, it didn't feel right. It didn't feel right. The first sign, as President Hennessy was saying, was when they tried to change my name. The news director said to me at the time, "Nobody's going to remember Oprah. So, we want to change your name. We've come up with a name we think that people will remember and people will like. Its a friendly name: Suzie."

Hi, Suzie. Very friendly. You can't be angry with Suzie. Remember Suzie. But my name wasn't Suzie. And, you know, I'd grown up not really loving my name, because when you're looking for your little name on the lunch boxes and the license plate tags, you're never going to find Oprah.

So, I grew up not loving the name, but once I was asked to change it, I thought, well, it is my name and do I look like a Suzie to you? So, I thought, no, it doesn't feel right. I'm not going to change my name. And if people remember it or not, that's OK.

And then they said they didn't like the way I looked. This was in 1976, when your boss could call you in and say, "I don't like the way you look." Now that would be called a lawsuit, but back then they could just say, "I don't like the way you look." Which, in case some of you in the back, if you can't tell, is nothing like Barbara Walters. So, they sent me to a salon where they gave me a perm, and after a few days all my hair fell out and I had to shave my head. And then they really didn't like the way I looked.

Because now I am black and bald and sitting on TV. Not a pretty picture.

But even worse than being bald, I really hated, hated, hated being sent to report on other people's tragedies as a part of my daily duty, knowing that I was just expected to observe, when everything in my instinct told me that I should be doing something, I should be lending a hand.

So. as President Hennessy said, I'd cover a fire and then I'd go back and I'd try to give the victims blankets. And I wouldn't be able to sleep at night because of all the things I was covering during the day.

And, meanwhile, I was trying to sit gracefully like Barbara and make myself talk like Barbara. And I thought, well, I could make a pretty goofy Barbara. And if I could figure out how to be myself, I could be a pretty good Oprah. I was trying to sound elegant like Barbara. And sometimes I didn't read my copy, because something inside me said, this should be spontaneous. So, I wanted to get the news as I was giving it to the people. So, sometimes, I wouldn't read my copy and it would be, like, six people on a pileup[1] on I-40. Oh, my goodness.

And sometimes I wouldn't read the copy—because I wanted to be spontaneous—and I'd come across a list of words I didn't know and I'd mispronounce. And one day I was reading copy and I called Canada "ca nada." And I decided, this Barbara thing's not going too well. I should try being myself.

1. A pileup: a massive collision of several or many moving vehicles.

But at the same time, my dad was saying, "Oprah Gail, this is an opportunity of a lifetime. You better keep that job." And my boss was saying, "This is the nightly news. You're an anchor, not a social worker. Just do your job."

So, I was juggling these messages of expectation and obligation and feeling really miserable with my self. I'd go home at night and fill up my journals, 'cause I've kept a journal since I was 15—so I now have volumes of journals. So I'd go home at night and fill up my journals about how miserable I was and frustrated. Then I'd eat my anxiety. That's where I learned that habit.

And after eight months, I lost that job. They said I was too emotional. I was too much. But since they didn't want to pay out the contract, they put me on a talk show in Baltimore. And the moment I sat down on that show, the moment I did, I felt like I'd come home. I realized that TV could be more than just a playground, but a platform for service, for helping other people lift their lives. And the moment I sat down, doing that talk show, it felt like breathing. It felt right. And that's where everything that followed for me began.

And I got that lesson. When you're doing the work you're meant to do, it feels right and every day is a bonus, regardless of what you're getting paid.

It's true. And how do you know when you're doing something right? How do you know that? It feels so. What I know now is that feelings are really your GPS system for life. When you're supposed to do something or not supposed to do something, your emotional guidance system lets you know. The trick is to learn to check your ego at the door and start checking your gut instead. Every right decision I've made—every right decision I've ever made—has come from my gut. And every wrong decision I've ever made was a result of me not listening to the greater voice of myself.

If it doesn't feel right, don't do it. That's the lesson. And that lesson alone will save you, my friends, a lot of grief. Even doubt means don't. This is what I've learned. There are many times when you don't know what to do. When you don't know what to do, get still, get very still, until you do know what to do.

And when you do get still and let your internal motivation be the driver, not only will your personal life improve, but you will gain a competitive edge[1] in the working world as well. Because, as Daniel Pink writes in his best-seller, A Whole New Mind, we're entering a whole new age. And he calls it the Conceptual Age, where traits that set people apart today are going to come from our hearts—right brain—as well as our heads. It's no longer just the logical, linear, rules-based thinking that matters, he says. It's also empathy and joyfulness and purpose, inner traits that have transcendent worth.

These qualities bloom when we're doing what we love, when we're involving the wholeness of ourselves in our work, both our expertise and our emotion.

So, I say to you, forget about the fast lane. If you really want to fly, just harness your power to your passion. Honor your calling. Everybody has one. Trust your heart and success will come to you.

So, how do I define success? Let me tell you, money's pretty nice. I'm not going to stand up here and tell you that it's not about money, 'cause money is very nice. I like money. It's good for buying things.

But having a lot of money does not automatically make you a successful person. What you want is money and meaning. You want your work to be meaningful. Because meaning is what brings the real richness to your life. What you really want is to be surrounded by people you trust and treasure and by people who cherish you. That's when you're really rich.

---

1. If you say that someone or something has an edge. you mean that they have a powerful quality.

So, lesson one, follow your feelings. If it feels right, move forward. If it doesn't feel right, don't do it.

Now I want to talk a little bit about failings, because nobody's journey is seamless or smooth. We all stumble. We all have setbacks. If things go wrong, you hit a dead end—as you will—it's just life's way of saying time to change course. So, ask every failure—this is what I do with every failure, every crisis, every difficult time—I say, what is this here to teach me? And as soon as you get the lesson, you get to move on. If you really get the lesson, you pass and you don't have to repeat the class. If you don't get the lesson, it shows up wearing another pair of pants—or skirt—to give you some remedial work.

And what I've found is that difficulties come when you don't pay attention to life's whisper, because life always whispers to you first. And if you ignore the whisper, sooner or later you'll get a scream. Whatever you resist persists. But, if you ask the right question—not why is this happening, but what is this here to teach me?—it puts you in the place and space to get the lesson you need.

My friend Eckhart Tolle, who's written this wonderful book called A New Earth that's all about letting the awareness of who you are stimulate everything that you do, he puts it like this: He says, don't react against a bad situation; merge with that situation instead. And the solution will arise from the challenge. Because surrendering yourself doesn't mean giving up; it means acting with responsibility.

Many of you know that, as President Hennessy said, I started this school in Africa. And I founded the school, where I'm trying to give South African girls a shot at a future like yours—Stanford. And I spent five years making sure that school would be as beautiful as the students. I wanted every girl to feel her worth reflected in her surroundings. So, I checked every blueprint, I picked every pillow. I was looking at the grout[1] in between the

1. Grout is a thin mixture of sand, water, and cement or lime, which is used to

bricks. I knew every thread count of the sheets. I chose every girl from the villages, from nine provinces. And yet, last fall, I was faced with a crisis I had never anticipated. I was told that one of the dorm matrons[1] was suspected of sexual abuse.

That was, as you can imagine, devastating news. First, I cried—actually, I sobbed—for about half an hour. And then I said, let's get to it; that's all you get, a half an hour. You need to focus on the now, what you need to do now. So, I contacted a child trauma specialist. I put together a team of investigators. I made sure the girls had counseling and support. And Gayle and I got on a plane and flew to South Africa.

And the whole time I kept asking that question: What is this here to teach me? And, as difficult as that experience has been, I got a lot of lessons. I understand now the mistakes I made, because I had been paying attention to all of the wrong things. I'd built that school from the outside in, when what really mattered was the inside out.

So, it's a lesson that applies to all of our lives as a whole. What matters most is what's inside. What matters most is the sense of the integrity, of quality and beauty. I got that lesson. And what I know is that the girls came away with something, too. They have emerged from this more resilient and knowing that their voices have power.

And their resilience and spirit have given me more than I could ever give to them, which leads me to my final lesson—the one about finding happiness—which we could talk about all day, but I know you have other wacky[2] things to do.

Not a small topic this is, finding happiness. But in some ways I think it's the simplest of all. Gwendolyn Brooks wrote a poem

---

fill in the space between titles that are fixed to a wall.

1. The matrom in a mursing home is the woman who is in charge of all the nurses.
2. If you describe something or someone as wacky, you mean that they are eccentric, unusual, and often funny.

for her children. It's called "Speech to the Young : Speech to the Progress-Toward." And she says at the end, "Live not for battles won. / Live not for the-end-of-the-song. / Live in the along." She's saying, like Eckhart Tolle, that you have to live for the present. You have to be in the moment. Whatever has happened to you in your past has no power over this present moment, because life is now.

But I think she's also saying, be a part of something. Don't live for yourself alone. This is what I know for sure: In order to be truly happy, you must live along with and you have to stand for something larger than yourself. Because life is a reciprocal exchange. To move forward you have to give back. And to me, that is the greatest lesson of life. To be happy, you have to give something back.

I know you know that, because that's a lesson that's woven into the very fabric of this university. It's a lesson that Jane and Leland Stanford got and one they've bequeathed to you. Because all of you know the story of how this great school came to be, how the Stanfords lost their only child to typhoid at the age of 15. They had every right and they had every reason to turn their backs against the world at that time, but instead, they channeled their grief and their pain into an act of grace. Within a year of their son's death, they had made the founding grant[1] for this great school, pledging to do for other people's children what they were not able to do for their own boy.

The lesson here is clear, and that is, if you're hurting, you need to help somebody ease their hurt. If you're in pain, help somebody else's pain. And when you're in a mess, you get yourself out of the mess helping somebody out of theirs. And in the process, you get to become a member of what I call the greatest fellowship[2] of all, the sorority of compassion and the

1. A grant as an amount of money that a government or other institution gives to an individual or to an organization for a particular purpose such as education or home improvements. • They'd got a special grant to encourage research.
2. Fellowship is a feeling of friendship that people have when they are talking

fraternity of service.

The Stanfords had suffered the worst thing any mom and dad can ever endure, yet they understood that helping other is the way we help ourselves. And this wisdom is increasingly supported by scientific and sociological research. It's no longer just woo-woo soft-skills[1] talk. There's actually a helper's high, a spiritual surge you gain from serving other. So, if you want to feel good, you have to go out and do some good.

But when you do good, I hope you strive for more than just the good feeling that service provides, because I know this for sure, that doing good actually makes you better. So, whatever field you choose, if you operate from the paradigm of service, I know your life will have more value and you will be happy.

I was always happy doing my talk show, but that happiness reached a depth of fulfillment, of joy, that I really can't describe to you or measure when I stopped just being on TV and looking at TV as a job and decided to use television, to use it and not have it use me, to use it as a platform to serve my viewers. That alone changed the trajectory of my success.

So, I know this—that whether you're an actor, you offer your talent in the way that most inspires art. If you're an anatomist, you look at your gift as knowledge and service to healing. Whether you've been called, as so many of you here today getting doctorates and other degrees, to the professions of business, law, engineering, humanities, science, medicine, if you choose to offer your skills and talent in service, when you choose the paradigm of service, looking at life through that paradigm, it turns everything you do from a job into a gift. And I know you haven't spent all the time at Stanford just to go out and get a job.

You've been enriched in countless ways. There's no better way

---

or doing something together and sharing their experiences.(= companionship)

1. Soft skills are interpersonal skills as the ability to communicate well with other people and to work in a team.

to make your mark[1] on the world and to share that abundance with others. My constant prayer for myself is to be used in service for the greater good.

So, let me end with one of my favorite quotes from Martin Luther King. Dr. King said, "Not everybody can be famous." And I don't know, but everybody today seems to want to be famous.

But fame is a trip. People follow you to the bathroom, listen to you pee. It's just—try to pee quietly. It doesn't matter, they come out and say, "Ohmigod, it's you. You peed."

That's the fame trip, so I don't know if you want that.

So, Dr King said, "Not everybody can be famous. But everybody can be great, because greatness is determined by service." Those of you who are history scholars may know the rest of that passage. He said, "You don't have to have a college degree to serve. You don't have to make your subject and verb agree to serve. You don't have to know about Plato or Aristotle to serve. You don't have to know Einstein's theory of relativity to serve. You don't have to know the second theory of thermodynamics in physics to serve. You only need a heart full of grace and a soul generated by love."

In a few moments, you'll all be officially Stanford's '08.

You have the heart and the smarts to go with it. And it's up to you to decide, really, where will you now use those gift? You've got the diploma, so go out and get the lesson, 'cause I know great things are sure to come.

You know, I've always believed that everything is better when you share it, so before I go, I wanted to share a graduation gift with you. Underneath your seats you'll find two of my favorite books. Eckhart Tolle's A New Earth is my current book club

1. If you make your mark or make a mark, you become noticed or famous by doing something impressive or unusual.

selection. Our *New Earth* webcast has been downloaded 30 million times with that book. And Daniel Pink's *A whole new mind: Why Right-Brainers Will Rule the Future* has reassured me I'm in the right direction.

I really wanted to give you cars but I just couldn't pull that off! Congratulations, '08!

Thank you. Thank you

After You Read

1. Oprah Winfrey is talking about the secret she has learned to getting ahead. What is it?

2. She thinks about one of the greatest compliments she's ever received. Would you explain?

3. She knows that money is more precious than inner wisdom. Is that true?

4. What are the three lessons that have had the greatest impact on her life?

5. According to Ophra, when you're doing the work you're meant to do, how does it feel?

6. According to Ophra, when you don't pay attention to life's whisper. what happens?

7. In order to be truly happy. what do you have to do?

3

How to Read Body Language

by David Abercrombie

All of us communicate with one another nonverbally, as well as with words. Most of the time we're not aware that we're doing it. We gesture with eyebrows or a hand, meet someone else's eyes and look away, shift position in a chair. These action we assume are random and incidental[1]. But researchers have discovered in recent years that there is a system to them almost as consistent and comprehensible as language.

Every culture has its own body language, and children absorb its nuances[2] along with spoken language. A Frenchman talks and moves in French. The way an Englishman crosses his legs is nothing like the way a male American does it. In talking, Americans are apt to end a statement with a droop[3] of the head or hand, a lowering of the eyelids. They wind up[4] a question with a lift of the hand, a tilt of the chin or a widening of the eyes. With a future-tense verb they often gesture with a forward movement.

There are regional idioms too; an expert can sometimes pick out a native of Wisconsin just by the way he uses his eyebrows during conversation. Your sex, ethnic background, social class and personal style all influence your body language. Nevertheless, you move and gesture within your national idiom. The person who

1. incidental: occurring merely by chance or without intention or calculation
2. nuance: a slight or delicate variation in tone, color, meaning, etc.; shade of difference
3. droop: downward deflection; the condition or appearance of drooping
4. wind up: ~을 끝마치고, ~을 마무리 짓다

is truly bilingual is also bilingual in body language. New York's famous mayor, Fiorello La Guardia, politicked in English, Italian and Yiddish[1]. When films of his speeches are run without sound, it's not too difficult to identify from his gestures the language he was speaking. One of the reasons English-dubbed[2] foreign films often seem flat is that the gestures don't match the language.

Usually, the wordless communication acts to qualify[3] the words. What the nonverbal elements express very often, and very efficiently, is the emotional side of the message. When a person feels liked or disliked, often it's a case of "not what he said but the way he said it." Psychologist Albert Mehrabian has devised this formula: total impact of a message=7 percent verbal+38 percent vocal+55 percent facial. The importance of the voice can be seen when you consider that even the words "I hate you" can be made to sound sexy.

Experts in kinetics[4]—the study of communication through body movement—are not prepared to spell out a precise vocabulary of gestures. When an American rubs his nose, it may mean he is disagreeing with someone or rejecting something. But there are other possible interpretations, too. Another example: when a student in conversation with a professor holds the older man's eyes a little longer than is usual, it can be a sign of respect and affection; it can be a subtle challenge to the professor's authority; or it can be something else entirely. The expert looks for patterns in the context, not for an isolated meaningful gesture.

Kinetics is a young science—about 17 years old—and very much the brainchild[5] of one man, anthropologist Dr. Ray L. Birdwhistell. But it already offers a wide variety of small observations. (For example: eyebrows have a repertoire[6] of

---

1. Yiddish: a language derived from Middle High German, spoken by East European Jews and their descendants in other countries
2. dub: to insert in (a film) a soundtrack with synchronized dialogue in another language
3 qualify: to moderate; soften
4. kinetics: the study of bodily movements, facial expressions, etc. as ways of communication or as accompaniments to speech
5. brainchild: an idea, plan, etc. regarded as produced by a person's own mental labor
6. repertoire: the stock of special skills, devices, techniques, etc. of a particular person or particular field of endeavor

about 23 possible positions; men use their eyebrows more than women do.) Most people find they can shut out conversation and concentrate on watching body language for only about 30 seconds at a time. Anyone can experiment with it, however, simply by turning on the television picture without the sound. One of the most potent elements in body language is eye behavior. Americans are careful about how and when they meet one another's eyes. In our normal conversation, each eye contact lasts only about a second before one or both individuals look away. When two Americans look searchingly into each other's eyes, emotions are heightened and the relationship becomes more intimate. Therefore, we carefully avoid this, except in appropriate circumstances.

Americans abroad sometimes find local eye behavior hard to interpret. "Tel Aviv was disturbing," one man recalled. "People stared right at me on the street; they looked me up and down. I kept wondering if I was uncombed or unzipped. Finally, a friend explained that Israelis think nothing of staring at others on the street."

Proper street behavior in the United States requires a nice balance of attention and inattention. You are supposed to look at a passerby just enough to show that you're aware of his presence. If you look too little, you appear haughty or secretive; too much, and you were inquisitive. Usually what happens is that people eye each other until they are about eight feet apart, at which point both cast down their eyes. Sociologist Dr. Erving Goffman describes this as "a kind of dimming[1] of lights." In parts of the Far East it is impolite to look at the other person at all during conversation. In England polite listener stares at the speaker attentively and blinks his eyes occasionally as a sign of interest. That eye-blink says nothing to Americans, who expect the listener to nod or to murmur something—such as "mm-hmm."

There are times when what a person says with his body gives the lie to[2] what he is saying with his tongue. Sigmund Freud once wrote: "No mortal[3] can keep a secret. If his lips are silent, he chatters with his fingertips; betrayal oozes out of him

1 dim: to turn (headlights) down by switching from high to low beam

2 give the lie to: ~이 거짓이라는 것을 나타내다; ~에 반하다, 모순되다

3. mortal: a being who must eventually die; esp., a human being; person

at every pore. "Thus, a man may successfully control his face, and appear calm, self-controlled—unaware that signs of tension and anxiety are leaking out, that his foot is beating the floor constantly, restlessly, as if it had a life of its own. Rage is another emotion feet and legs may reveal. During arguments the feet often become tense. Fear sometimes produces barely perceptible running motions, a kind of nervous leg jiggle[1]. Then there are the subtle, provocative leg gestures that women use, consciously and unconsciously.

Recent studies by psychologists suggests that posture often reflects a person's attitude toward people he is with. One experiment indicates that when men are with other men they dislike, they relax either very little or very much—depending on whether they see the other man as threatening. Women in this experiment always signaled dislike with very relaxed posture. And men, paired with women they disliked, were never tense enough about it to sit rigidly.

Posture sometimes offer a guide to broad relationship within a group. Imagine that at a party, guests have been fired up by an argument over student radicalism. You may be able to spot[2] at a glance the two sides of argument by postures adopted. Most of the pros, for example, may sit with crossed knees, the cons with legs stretched out and arms folded. A few middle-of-the-roaders[3] may try a little of each—crossing their knees and folding their arms. If an individual abruptly shifts his body around in his chair, it may mean that he disagrees with the speaker or even that he is changing sides. None of this, of course, represents an infallible guide, but it is apparently significant enough to be worth watching for.

While children learn spoken and body language—proper postures, eye behavior, etc.—they also learn a subtler thing: how to react to space around them. Man walks round inside a kind of private bubble, which represents the amount of air space he feels he must have between himself and other people. Anthropologists, working with cameras, have recorded the tremors and minute

1. jiggle: a jiggling movement 위아래(앞뒤)로의 빠른 움직임; 흔들림
2 spot: to pick out; detect; see; recognize
3 middle-of-the-roader: one that stands midway between extremes (as in opinions)

eye movements that betray the moment the individual's bubble is breached[1]. As adults, however, we hide our feelings behind a screen of polite words.

Anthropologist Dr. Edward T. Hall points out that, for two unacquainted adult male North American, the comfortable distance to stand for private conversation is from arm's length to about four feet apart. The South American likes to stand much closer, which creates problems when the two meet face to face. For, as the South American moves in, the North American feels he's being pushy[2]: and as the North American backs off the South American thinks he's being standoffish[3].

The American and the Arab are even less compatible in their space habits. Arabs like close contact. In some instances, they stand very close together to talk, staring intently[4] into each other's eyes and breathing into each other's face. These are actions the American may associate with sexual intimacy and he may find it disturbing to be subjected to them in a nonsexual context.

The amount of space a man needs is also influenced by his personality—introverts, for example, seem to need more elbowroom than extroverts. Situation and mood also affects distance. Movie-goers waiting in line to see a sexy film will line up much more densely than those waiting to see a family-entertainment movie.

George du Maurier once wrote: "Language is a poor thing. You fill your lungs with wind and shake a little slit in your throat and make mouths, and that shakes the air; and air shakes a pair of little drums in my head...and my brain seize your meaning in the rough[5]. What a roundabout [6]way and a waste of time!"

Communication between human beings would be just that dull if it were all done with words. But actually, words are often the smallest part of it.

1. breach: to make a breach in; break open or through ~을 깨뜨리다, 돌파하다
2. pushy: annoyingly aggressive and persistent 주제넘게 나서는
3. standoffish: reserved and cool; aloof
4 intently: in an intent manner 열심히
5 in the rough: 대충(의), 대략(의)
6. roundabout: not straight or straight forward; indirect; circuitous 우회적인, 간접적인

AFTER YOU READ

1. In talking, how are Americans apt to end a statement?

2. What do nonverbal elements express very often, and very efficiently?

3. What does an American mean when he rubs his nose?

4. How long does eye contact last in our normal conversation?

5. If an individual abruptly shifts his body around in his chair, what does he mean?

6. Which people are even less compatible in their space habits?

4

UNIVERSITIES HAVE FALLEN[1] DOWN ON THE JOB OF TEACHING VALUES

By James Billington

To a very large extent, American universities have fallen down on the job of transmitting values to students. Other institutions are also falling short, but the universities' failure is especially serious because historically they have had the task of imparting[2] the essentials of the Western tradition to the leaders of tomorrow. Now young people in universities are generally offered a smorgasbord[3] curriculum that fails to convey any sense of their own heritage. There has been a decline in faculty with a commitment to traditional values. As a consequence, universities do not provide young people with role models.

All of this occurred because major research universities became dedicated to specialization somewhat in imitation of the industrial process on the assembly line, where everyone has a specialized function. While you can produce a whole car through specialization, you cannot produce a whole person that way. And without whole people who have strong civic involvement and deep personal convictions and commitments, democracy cannot function.

If we are going to be together as a people, we have to have a higher-educational process that puts at least a few things back[4] together. Instead, we have a consumer-oriented curriculum that

1. fall down: 실패하다
2. impart: to make known; tell; reveal
3. smorgasbord: any widely varied assortment or collection
4. put back: 되돌려주다, 되돌려 놓다

refuses even to make judgments that Shakespeare is more worth reading than Sartre[1] or that the Bible is more worth knowing than Nietzsche[2].

The failure of the universities to transmit traditional values has left the field wide open to ideologies and methodologies—those modern substitutes for religion. Certain points of view accepted in academic guilds[3] have become the values transmitted by higher education. School impart values under the guise of imparting none. That is a form of dishonesty corrosive of a healthy democracy, which requires a pluralism of values contesting in an open market rather than the pretense of no values at all.

In history, for example, the prevailing mode of thought suggests that people's actions are not the result of conscious moral choice but of a combination of socioeconomic pressure and psychosexual[4] drives. This conveys a sense that history is made by broad, impersonal forces—a perspective that diminishes the importance of individual choice and of the moral component in that choice. There's a tendency to see things in a deterministic way and not to study what is most human about people—their anguish, achievements and aspirations. This view of people helps make us a less caring society and may also play a role in the decreasing enthusiasm for politics.

Universities often unintentionally convey to young people the sense that self-indulgence is not only permissible but even desirable. As schools have done away with the old-fashioned view of acting in place of parents on matters of morality, they have become totally permissive sexually. Young people acquire an unreal sense of freedom—all the privileges of adults with none of the responsibilities. No one—least of all deans or chaplains[5]—speaks out prominently for self-discipline. The emphasis is on adjusting to, understanding and accepting the student's right to do

---

1. Sartre: Jean Paul S~(1905~1980) 프랑스의 소설가, 극작가
2. Nietzsche: Friedrich N~(1844~1900) 19세기 독일의 철학자
3. guild: any association for mutual and the promotion of common interests 협회
4. psychosexual: of or having to do with the psychological aspects of sexuality in contrast to the physical aspects 성심리적인
5. chaplain: a minister, priest, rabbi serving in a religious capacity with the armed forces, or in a prison, hospital, etc.

this or that.

Granted that the old restrictions and rules may have been difficult to enforce—and some may have been unduly repressive—but you cannot bring together thousands of adolescents and have neither role models nor proclamation of standards. With no one publicly defining a norm, the modern university drifts into a kind of conformist nonconformism. As a consequence, universities end up producing, on the whole, very lonely people held together more by animal ritual than by a sense of richer human community.

One of the worst things about higher education today is that it induces[1] a profound cynicism that often descends into apathy about learning itself. There is so much intense reading, analysis and writing at high-pressure research universities that people are often turned off[2] from serious use of their minds for the rest of their lives. By setting up this kind of intense assembly line for four years of college and then a few years of professional school, we are in effect, saying that we are training machines, not training citizens for a democracy.

Because of all of these developments, we are seeing a growing split between those who are morally concerned but not intellectually trained and those who are highly articulate[3] but morally insensitive. That is very serious for democracy: It may not survive a full generation of that kind of polarization. That's why it's important to get basic moral standards and commitment back into the highest levels of our intellectual effort. After all, it was the combination of spiritual, moral and civic concerns with exacting intellectual activity that really built this country and made democracy work on a continental scale.

1. induce: to bring on; bring about; cause; effect
2. turn off: 흥미를 잃다
3. articulate: expressing oneself easily and clearly; well formulated; cleary presented

AFTER YOU READ

1. Why do American universities fail to convey any sense of their own heritage?

2. What does a healthy democracy require?

3. What helps make us a less caring society?

4. What does modern university drift into, with no one publicly defining a norm?

5. What are they training by setting up this kind of intense assembly line for four years of college and then a few years of professional school?

5

Barack Obama: Nobel Peace Prize Acceptance Speech Dec. 12, 2009. Oslo, Norway

by Barack Obama

Your Majesties, Your Royal Highnesses, Distinguished Members of the Norwegian Nobel Committee, citizens of America, and citizens of the world:

I receive this honor with deep gratitude and great humility. It is an award that speaks to our highest aspirations—that for all the cruelty and hardship of our world, we are not mere prisoners of fate. Our actions matter, and can bend history in the direction of justice.

And yet I would be remiss[1] if I did not acknowledge the considerable controversy that your generous decision has generated. In part, this is because I am at the beginning, and not the end, of my labors on the world stage. Compared to some of the giants of history who have received this prize—Schweitzer and King; Marshall and Mandela—my accomplishments are slight. And then there are the men and women around the world who have been jailed and beaten in the pursuit of justice; those who toil in humanitarian organizations to relieve suffering; the unrecognized millions whose quiet acts of courage and compassion inspire even the most hardened of cynics. I cannot argue with those who find these men and women—some known, some obscure to all but those they help—to be far more deserving

1. If someone is remiss, they are careless about doing things which ought to be done. • I would be remiss if I did not do something about it.

of this honor than I.

But perhaps the most profound issue surrounding my receipt of this prize is the fact that I am the Commander-in-Chief of a nation in the midst of two wars. One of these wars is winding down. The other is a conflict that America did not seek; one in which we are joined by 43 other countries—including Norway—in an effort to defend ourselves and all nations from further attacks.

Still, we are at war, and I am responsible for the deployment of thousands of young Americans to battle in a distant land. Some will kill. Some will be killed. And so I come here with an acute sense of the cost of armed conflict—filled with difficult questions about the relationship between war and peace, and our effort to replace one with the other.

These questions are not new. War, in one form or another, appeared with the first man. At the dawn of history, its morality was not questioned; it was simply a fact, like drought or disease—the manner in which tribes and then civilizations sought power and settled their differences.

Over time, as codes of law sought to control violence within groups, so did philosophers, clerics and statesmen seek to regulate the destructive power of war. The concept of a "just war" emerged, suggesting that war is justified only when it meets certain preconditions: if it is waged as a last resort or in self-defense; if the forces used is proportional; and if, whenever possible, civilians are spared from violence.

For most of history, this concept of just war was rarely observed. The capacity of human beings to think up new ways to kill one another proved inexhaustible, as did our capacity to exempt from mercy[1] those who look different or pray to a different God. Wars between armies gave way to wars between nations—total wars in which the distinction between combatant and civilian became blurred. In the span of 30 years, such carnage

---

1. exempt from mercy : 가혹하게 대하다.

would twice engulf this continent. And while it is hard to conceive of a cause more just than the defeat of the Third Reich and the Axis powers, World War II was a conflict in which the total number of civilians who died exceeded the number of soldiers who perished.

In the wake of such destruction, and with the advent of the nuclear age, it became clear to victor and vanquished alike that the world needed institutions to prevent another World War. And so, a quarter century after the United States Senate rejected the League of Nation—an idea for which Woodrow Wilson received this Prize—America led the world in constructing an architecture to keep the peace: a Marshall Plan and a United Nations, mechanisms to govern the waging of war, treaties to protect human rights, prevent genocide and restrict the most dangerous weapons.

In many ways, these efforts succeeded. Yes, terrible wars have been fought, and atrocities committed. But there has been no Third World War. The Cold War ended with jubilant crowds dismantling a wall. Commerce has stitched much of the world together. Billions have been lifted from poverty. The ideals of liberty, self-determination, equality and the rule of law have haltingly advanced. We are the heirs of the fortitude and foresight of generations past, and it is a legacy for which my own county is rightfully proud.

A decade into a new century, this old architecture is buckling[1] under the weight of new threats. The world may no longer shudder at the prospect of war between two nuclear superpowers, but proliferation may increase the risk of catastrophe. Terrorism has long been a tactic, but modern technology allows a few small men with outsized[2] rage to murder innocents on a horrific scale.

Moreover, wars between nations have increasingly given way

1. If an object buckles or if something buckles it, it becomes bent as a result of very great heat or force.
2. Outsize or outsized things are much larger than usual or much larger than you would expect.

to wars within nations. The resurgence of ethnic or sectarian conflicts, the growth of secessionist movements, insurgencies and failed states have increasingly trapped civilians in unending chaos. In today's wars, many more civilians are killed than soldiers; the seeds of future conflict are sown, economies are wrecked, civil societies torn asunder, refugees amassed[1] and children scarred.

I do not bring with me today a definitive solution to the problems of war. What I do know is that meeting these challenges will require the same vision, hard work and persistence of those men and women who acted so boldly decades ago. And it will require us to think in new ways about the notions of just war and the imperatives of a just peace.

We must begin by acknowledging the hard truth that we will not eradicate violent conflict in our lifetimes. There will be times when nation—acting individually or in concert—will find the use of force not only necessary but morally justified.

I make this statement mindful[2] of what Martin Luther King said in this same ceremony years ago: "Violence never brings permanent peace. It solves no social problem: It merely creates new and more complicated ones." As someone who stands here as a direct consequence of Dr. King's life's work, I am living testimony to the moral force of non-violence. I know there is nothing weak, nothing passive, nothing naive in the creed and lives of Gandhi and King.

But as a head of state sworn to protect and defend my nation, I cannot be guided by their examples alone. I face the world as it is, and cannot stand idle in the face of threats to the American people. For make no mistake: Evil does exist in the world. A nonviolent movement could not have halted Hitler's armies. Negotiations cannot convince al-Qaida's leaders to lay down their arms. To say that force is sometimes necessary is not a call to cynicism—it is a recognition of history, the imperfections of man

---

1. If you amass something such as money or information, you gradually get a lot of it. • How had he amassed his fortune? (=accrue, accumulate)
2. mindful of : 염두에 두는, 잊지 않는

and the limits of reason.

I raise this point because in many countries there is a deep ambivalence about military action today, no matter the cause. At times, this is joined by a reflexive suspicion of America, the world's sole military superpower.

Yet the world must remember that it was not simply international institutions—not just treaties and declarations—that brought stability to a post-World War II world. Whatever mistakes we have made, the plain fact is this: The United States of America has helped underwrite[1] global security for more than six decades with the blood of our citizens and the strength of our arms. The service and sacrifice of our men and women in uniform has promoted peace and prosperity from Germany to Korea, and enabled democracy to take hold in places like the Balkans. We have borne this burden not because we seek to impose our will. We have done so out of enlightened self-interest—because we seek a better future for our children and grandchildren, and we believe that their lives will be better if other people's children and grandchildren can live in freedom and prosperity.

So yes, the instruments of war do have a role to play in preserving the peace. And yet this truth must coexist with another—that no matter how justified, war promises human tragedy. The soldier's courage and sacrifice is full of glory, expressing devotion to country, to cause and to comrades in arms. But war itself is never glorious, and we must never trumpet it as such.

So part of our challenge is reconciling these two seemingly irreconcilable truths—that war is sometimes necessary, and war is at some level an expression of human folly. Concretely, we must direct our effort to the task that President Kennedy called

1. If an institution or company underwrites an activity or underwrites the cost of it, they agree to provide any money that is needed to cover losses or buy special equipment, often for an agreed fee.

for long ago. "Let us focus," he said, "on a more practical, more attainable peace, based not on a sudden revolution in human nature but on a gradual evolution in human institutions." What might this evolution look like? What might these practical steps be?

To begin with, I believe that all nations—strong and weak alike—must adhere to standards that govern the use of force. I—like any head of state—reserve the right to act unilaterally if necessary to defend my nation. Nevertheless, I am convinced that adhering to standards strengthens those who do, and isolates—and weakens—those who don't.

The world rallied around America after the 9/11 attacks, and continues to support our efforts in Afghanistan, because of the horror of those senseless attacks and the recognized principle of self-defense. Likewise, the world recognized the need to confront Saddam Hussein when he invaded Kuwait—a consensus that sent a clear message to all about the cost of aggression.

Futhermore, America cannot insist that others follow the rules of the road if we refuse to follow them ourselves. For when we don't, our action can appear arbitrary, and undercut the legitimacy of future intervention—no matter how justified.

This becomes particularly important when the purpose of military action extends beyond self-defense or the defense of one nation against an aggressor. More and more, we all confront difficult questions about how to prevent the slaughter of civilians by their own government, or to stop a civil war whose violence and suffering can engulf an entire region.

I believe that force can be justified on humanitarian grounds, as it was in the Balkans, or in other places that have been scarred by war. Inaction tears at[1] our conscience and can lead to more costly intervention later. That is why all responsible nations must

---

1. If a person or animal tears at something, they pull it violently and try to break it into pieces.

embrace the role that militaries with a clear mandate can play to keep the peace.

America's commitment to global security will never waver. But in a world in which threats are more diffuse, and missions more complex, America cannot act alone. This is true in Afghanistan. This is true in failed states like Somalia, where terrorism and piracy is joined by famine and human suffering. And sadly, it will continue to be true in unstable regions for years to come.

The leaders and soldiers of NATO countries—and other friends and allies—demonstrate this truth through the capacity and courage they have shown in Afghanistan. But in many countries, there is a disconnect between the efforts of those who serve and the ambivalence of the broader public. I understand why war is not popular. But I also know this: The belief that peace is desirable is rarely enough to achieve it. Peace requires responsibility. Peace entails sacrifice. That is why NATO continues to be indispensable. That is why we must strengthen U.N. and regional peacekeeping, and not leave the task to a few countries. That is why we honor those who return home from peacekeeping and training abroad to Oslo and Rome; to Ottawa and Sydney; to Dhaka and Kigali—we honor them not as makers of war, but as wagers[1] of peace.

Let me make one final point about the use of force. Even as we make difficult decisions about going to war, we must also think clearly about how we fight it. The Nobel Committee recognized this truth in awarding its first prize for peace to Henry Dunaut—the founder of the Red Cross, and a driving force behind the Geneva Conventions.

Where force is necessary, we have a moral and strategic interest in binding ourselves to certain rules of conduct. And even as we confront a vicious adversary that abide by no rules, I believe that the United States of America must remain a standard bearer in the conduct of war. That is what makes us different

1. wager; conductor : 수행자

from those whom we fight. That is a source of our strength. That is why I prohibited torture. That is why I ordered the prison at Guantanamo Bay closed. And that is why I have reaffirmed America's commitment to abide by the Geneva Conventions. We lose ourselves when we compromise the very ideals that we fight to defend. And we honor those ideals by upholding them not just when it is easy, but when it is hard.

I have spoken to the questions that must weigh on our minds and our hearts as we choose to wage war. But let me turn now to our effort to avoid such tragic choices, and speak of three ways that we can build a just and lasting peace.

First, in dealing with those nations that break rules and laws, I believe that we must develop alternatives to violence that are tough enough to change behavior—for if we want a lasting peace, then the words of the international community must mean something. Those regimes that break the rules must be held accountable. Sanctions must exact a real price. Intransigence[1] must be met with increased pressure—and such pressure exists only when the world stands together as one.

One urgent example is the effort to prevent the spread of nuclear weapons, and to seek a world without them. In the middle of the last century, nations agreed to be bound by a treaty whose bargain is clear: All will have access to peaceful nuclear power; those without nuclear weapons will forsake[2] them; and those with nuclear weapons will work toward disarmament. I am committed to upholding this treaty. It is a centerpiece of my foreign policy. And I am working with President Medvedev to reduce America and Russia's nuclear stockpiles.

But it is also incumbent upon all of us to insist that nations like Iran and North Korea do not game the system. Those who claim to respect international law cannot avert their eyes when

---

1. If you talk about someone's intransigence, you mean that they refuse to behave differently or to change their attitude to something.
2. forsake: give up

those laws are flouted[1]. Those who care for their own security cannot ignore the danger of an arms race in the Middle East or East Asia. Those who seek peace cannot stand idly by as nations arm themselves for nuclear war.

The same principle applies to those who violate international law by brutalizing their own people. When there is genocide in Darfur, systematic rape in Congo or repression in Burma—there must be consequences. And the closer we stand together, the less likely we will be faced with the choice between armed intervention and complicity in oppression.

This brings me to a second point—the nature of the peace that we seek. For peace is not merely the absence of visible conflict. Only a just peace based upon the inherent rights and dignity of every individual can truly be lasting.

It was this insight that drove drafters of the Universal Declaration of Human Rights after the Second World War. In the wake of[2] devastation, they recognized that if human rights are not protected, peace is a hollow promise.

And yet all too often, these words are ignored. In some countries, the failure to uphold human rights is excused by the false suggestion that these are Western principles, foreign to local cultures or stages of a nation's development. And within America, there has long been a tension between those who describe themselves as realists or idealists—a tension that suggests a stark choice between the narrow pursuit of interests or an endless campaign to impose our values.

I reject this choice. I believe that peace is unstable where citizens are denied the right to speak freely or worship as they

1. If you flout something such as law, an order, or an accepted way of behaving, you deliberately do not obey it. • illegal campers who persist in flouting the law.
2. If one thing follows in the wake of another, it happens after the other thing is over, often as a result of it. • The governor has enjoyed a huge surge in the polls in the wake of last weeks convention. (=following)

please, choose their own leaders or assemble without fear. Pent up[1] grievances fester, and the suppression of tribal and religious identity can lead to violence. We also know that the opposite is true. Only when Europe became free did it finally find peace. America has never fought a war against a democracy, and our closest friends are governments that protect the rights of their citizens. No matter how callously[2] defined, neither Americas's interests—nor the worlds—are served by the denial of human aspirations.

So even as we respect the unique culture and traditions of different countries, America will always be a voice for those aspirations that are universal. We will bear witness to the quiet dignity of reformers like Aung Sang Suu Kyi; to the bravery of Zimbabweans who cast their ballots in the face of beatings; to the hundreds of thousands who have marched silently through the streets of Iran. It is telling[3] that the leaders of these governments fear the aspirations of their own people more than the power of any other nation. And it is the responsibility of all free people and free nations to make clear to these movements that hope and history are on their side.

Let me also say this; The promotion of human rights cannot be about exhortation alone. At times, it must be coupled with painstaking diplomacy. I know that engagement with repressive regimes lacks the satisfying purity of indignation. But I also know that sanctions without outreach—and condemnation without discussion—can carry forward a crippling status quo. No repressive regime can move down a new path unless it has the choice of an open door.

In light of the Cultural Revolution's horrors, Nixon's meeting with Mao appeared inexcusable—and yet it surely helped set China on a path where millions of its citizens have been lifted from poverty, and connected to open societies. Pope John Paul's

1. pent up emotions, or forces have been held back and not expressed, used, or released. • He still had a lot of pent up anger to release.
2. callously : 냉담하게, 무정하게
3. telling : 명백한, 뚜렷한

engagement with Poland created space not just for the Catholic Church, but for labor leaders like Lech Walesa. Ronald Reagan's efforts on arms control and embrace of perestroika not only improved relations with the Soviet Union, but empowered dissidents throughout Eastern Europe. There is no simple formula here. But we must try as best we can to balance isolation and engagement, pressure and incentives, so that human rights and dignity are advanced over time.

Third, a just peace includes not only civil and political rights—it must encompass economic security and opportunity. For true peace is not just freedom from fear, but freedom from want.

It is undoubtedly true that development rarely takes root without security; it is also true that security does not exist where human beings do not have access to enough food, or clean water, or the medicine they need to survive. It does not exist where children cannot aspire to a decent education or a job that supports a family. The absence of hope can rot a society from within.

And that is why helping farmers feed their own people—or nations educate their children and care for the sick—is not mere charity. It is also why the world must come together to confront climate change. There is little scientific dispute that if we do nothing, we will face more drought, famine and mass displacement that will fuel more conflict for decades. For this reason, it is not merely scientists and activists who call for swift and forceful action—it is military leaders in my country and others who understand that our common security hangs in the balance[1].

Agreements among nations. Strong institutions. Support for human rights. Investments in development. All of these are vital ingredients in bringing about the evolution that President Kennedy spoke about. And yet, I do not believe that we will have the will, or the staying power, to complete this work

---

1. hangs in the balance : 어느 편으로 기울어질지 불안한 [미결정] 상태에 있다. [trembles]

without something more—and that is the continued expansion of our moral imagination, an insistence that there is something irreducible that we all share.

As the world grows smaller, you might think it would be easier for human beings to recognize how similar we are, to understand that we all basically want the same things, that we all hope for the chance to live out our lives with some measure of happiness and fulfillment for ourselves and our families.

And yet, given the dizzying pace of globalization, and the cultural leveling of modernity, it should come as no surprise that people fear the loss of what they cherish about their particular identities—their race, their tribe and, perhaps most powerfully, their religion. In some places, this fear has led to conflict. At times, it even feels like we are moving backwards. We see it in the Middle East, as the conflict between Arabs and Jews seems to harden. We see it in nations that are torn asunder by tribal lines.

Most dangerously, we see it in the way that religion is used to justify the murder of innocents by those who have distorted and defiled[1] the great religion of Islam, and who attacked my country from Afghanistan. These extremists are not the first to kill in the name of God; the cruelties of the Crusades are amply recorded. But they remind us that no Holy War can ever be a just war. For if you truly believe that you are carrying out divine will, then there is no need for restraint—no need to spare the pregnant mother, or the medic[2], or even a person of one's own faith. Such a warped view of religion is not just incompatible with the concept of peace, but the purpose of faith—for the one rule that lies at the heart of every major religion is that we do unto[3] others as we would have them do unto us.

Adhering to this law of love has always been the core struggle of human nature. We are fallible[4]. We make mistakes, and fall

---

1. defile : 신성모독하다
2. A medic is a doctor or medical student.
3. unto was used to indicate that something was done or given to someone. (=to)
4. If you say that someone or something is fallible, you mean that they are not

victim to the temptations of pride, and power, and sometimes evil. Even those of us with the best intentions will at times fail to right the wrongs before us.

But we do not have to think that human nature is perfect for us to still believe that the human condition can be perfected. We do not have to live in an idealized world to still reach for those ideals that will make it a better place. The nonviolence practiced by men like Gandhi and King may not have been practical or possible in every circumstance, but the love that they preached—their faith in human progress—must always be the North Star that guides us on our journey.

For if we lose that faith—if we dismiss it as silly or naive, if we divorce it from the decisions that we make on issues of war and peace—then we lose what is best about humanity. We lose our sense of possibility. We lose our moral compass.

Like generations have before us, we must reject that future. As Dr. King said at this occasion so many years ago: "I refuse to accept despair as the final response to the ambiguities of history. I refuse to accept the idea that the 'isness' of man's present nature makes him morally incapable of reaching up for the eternal 'oughtness' that forever confronts him."

So let us reach for the world that ought to be—that spark of the divine that still stirs within each of our souls. Somewhere today, in the here and now, a soldier sees he's outgunned[1] but stands firm to keep the peace. Somewhere today, in this world, stands firm to keep the peace. Somewhere today, in this world, a young protestor awaits the brutality of her government, but has the courage to march on. Somewhere today, a mother facing punishing poverty still takes the time to teach her child, who believes that a cruel world still has a place for his dreams.

---

perfect and are likely to make mistakes, or fail in what they are doing.

1. In a battle, if one army is outgunned, they are in a very weak position because the opposing army has more or better weapons.

Let us live by their example. We can acknowledge that oppression will always be with us, and still strive for justice. We can admit the intractability of deprivation, and still strive for dignity. We can understand that there will be war, and still strive for peace. We can do that—for that is the story of human progress; that is the hope of all the world; and at this moment of challenge, that must be our work here on Earth.

After You Read

1, Why does Mr. Obama refer to 'perhaps the most profound issue surrounding my receipt of this prize'?

2. By what did tribes and the civilizations seek power and settle their differences at the dawn of history?

3. What does Mr. Obama think about the creed and lives of Gandhi and King?

4. He says that a nonviolent movement and negotiations sometimes cannot work. Would you explain it?

5. The instruments of war do play a role. In what?

6. He speaks of three ways that we can build a just and lasting peace. What are they?

6

REPORT FROM EL DORADO

by Michael Ventura

Michael Ventura writes a column on popular culture and ideas for the L.A. Weekly. Some of these articles are collected in the 1985 book *shadow Dancing* in the U.S.A. For many Americans, watching television is simply a way to block out[1] the daily stress of work or school or personal problems. It might seem, then, that analyzing such a medium is to give it too much credit. It is, in fact, easy to dismiss most television programming as mere entertainment, but Ventura argues in the following article that we must pay attention to this medium, because "It *means* something to watch so much TV."

To go from a job you don't like to watching a screen on which others live more intensely than you ... is American life, by and large.

This is our political ground. This is our artistic ground. This is what we've done with our immense resources. We have to stop calling it "entertainment" or "news" or "sports" and start calling it what it is: our most immediate environment.

This is a very, very different America from the America that built the industrial capacity to win the Second World War and to surge forward on the multiple momentums of that victory for thirty years. That was an America that worked at mostly menial tasks during the day (now we work at mostly clerical tasks) and had to look at each other at night.

I'm not suggesting a nostalgia for that time. It was repressive

1. If someone block out a thought, they try not to think about it.

and bigoted to an extent that is largely forgotten today, to cite only two of its uglier aspects. But in that environment America meant *America*: the people and the land. The land was far bigger than what we'd done with the land.

This is no longer true. Now the environment of America is media. Not the land itself, but the image of the land. The focus is not on the people so much as it is on the interplay between people and screens. What we've done with the land is far more important now than the land—we're not even dealing with the land anymore, we're dealing with our manipulation and pollution of it.

And what we've done with the very concept of "image" is taking on far more importance for many of us than the actual sights and sounds of our lives.

For instance: Ronald Reagan stands on a cliff in Normandy to commemorate the day U.S. Army Rangers scaled those cliffs in the World War II invasion. Today's Rangers reenact the event while some of the original Rangers, in their sixties now, look on. Except that it is the wrong cliff. The cliff that was actually scaled is a bit further down the beach, but it's not as photogenic as this cliff, so this cliff has been chosen for everybody to emote over. Some of the old Rangers tell reporters that the historical cliff is over yonder, but the old Rangers are swept up (as well they might be) in the ceremonies, and nobody objects enough. This dislocation[1], this choice, this stance that the real cliff is not important, today's photograph is more important, is a media event. It insults the real event, and overpowers it. Multiplied thousands of times over thousands of outlets of every form and size, ensconced in textbooks as well as screenplays, in sales presentations as well as legislative packages, in religious revivals as well as performance-art[2] pieces, this is the process that has displaced[3] what used to be called "culture."

1. Dislocation is a situation in which something such as a system, process, or way of life is greatly disturbed or prevented from continuing as normal.
2. Performance art is a theatrical presentation that includes various art forms such as dance, music, painting, and sculpture.
3. If one thing displaces another, it forces the other thing out of its place, position, or role, and then occupies that place, position, or role itself.

"I'm not even sure it's a culture anymore. It's like this careening hunger splattering out in all directions."

Jeff Nightbyrd was trying to define "culture" in the wee hours at the Four Queens in Las Vegas. It was a conversation that had been going on since we'd become friends working on the *Austin Sun* in 1974, trying to get our bearings now that the sixties were *really over*. He'd spent that tripletime decade as an SDS organizer and editor of Rat, and I'd hit Austin after a few years of road-roving, commune-hopping, and intensive (often depressive) self-exploration—getting by, as the song said, with a little help from my friends, as a lot of us did then. This particular weekend Nightbyrd had come to Vegas from Austin for a computer convention, and I had taken off from my duties at the *L.A. Weekly* for some lessons in craps (at which Jeff is quite good) and to further our rap. The slot machines clattered around us in unison, almost comfortingly, the way the sound of a large shaky air-conditioner can be comforting in a cheap hotel room when you're trying to remember to forget. We were, after all, trying to fathom an old love: America.

There are worse places to indulge in this obsession than Las Vegas. It is the most American, the most audacious, of cities. Consuming unthinkable amounts of energy in the midst of an unlivable desert (Death Valley is not far away), its decor is based on various cheap-to-luxurious versions of a 1930s Busby Berkeley musical. Indeed, no studio backlot could ever be more of a set, teeming with extras, people who come from all over America, and all over the world, to see the topless, tasteless shows, the Johnny Carson guests on parade doing their utterly predictable routines, the dealers and crap-table croupiers who combine total boredom with ruthless efficiency and milk us dry—yet at least these tourists are risking something they genuinely value: money. It's a quiz show turned into a way of life, where you can get a good Italian dinner at dawn. Even the half-lit hour of the wolf doesn't faze[1] Las Vegas. How could it, when the town has survived the flash of atom bombs tested just over the horizon?

The history books will tell you that, ironically enough, the

1. If something fazes you, it surprises, shocks, or frightens you, so that you do not know what to do.

town was founded by Mormons in 1855. Even their purity of vision couldn't bear the intensity of this desert, and they abandoned the place after just two years. But they had left a human imprint, and a decade later the U.S. Army built a fort here. The settlement hung on[1], and the railroad came through in 1905. During the Second World War the Mafia started to build the city as we know it now. Religious zealots, the Army, and the Mafia—quite a triad of founding fathers.

Yet one could go back even further, some 400 years, when the first Europeans discovered the deserts of the American West—Spaniards who, as they slowly began to believe that there might be no end to these expansive wilds, became more and more certain that somewhere, somewhere to the north, lay El Dorado—a city of gold. Immeasurable wealth would be theirs, they believed, and eternal youth. What would they have thought if they had suddenly come upon modern Las Vegas, lying as it does in the midst of this bleached nowhere, glowing at night with a brilliance that would have frightened them? We have built our desert city to their measure—for they were gaudy and greedy, devout and vicious, jovial and frenzied, like this town. They had just wasted the entire Aztec civilization because their fantasies were so strong they couldn't see the ancient cultural marvels before their eyes. The Aztec, awed and terrified, believed they were being murdered by gods; and in the midst of such strangeness, the Spaniards took on godlike powers even in their own eyes. As many European would in America, they took liberties here they would never have taken within sight of their home cathedrals. Their hungers dominated them, and in their own eyes the New World seemed as inexhaustible as their appetites. So when Nightbyrd described our present culture as "a careening hunger splattering out in all directions," he was also, if unintentionally, speaking about our past. Fittingly, we were sitting in the midst of a city that had been fantasized by those seekers of El Dorado 400 years ago. In that sense, America had Las Vegas a century before it had Plymouth Rock. And our sensibility has been caught between the fantasies of the conquistadors and the obsessions of the Puritans ever since.

---

1. If you hang on, you manage to survive, achieve success, or avoid failure in spite of great difficulties or opposition.

Yes, a fitting place to try to think about American culture.

"There are memories of culture," Nightbyrd was saying, "but the things that have given people strength have dissolved. And because they're dissolved, people are into distractions. And distractions aren't culture."

Are there even memories? The media have taken over our memories. That day Nighbyrd had been driving through the small towns that dot this desert, towns for which Vegas is only a dull glow to the southwest. In a bar in one of those towns, "like that little bar in *The Right Stuff*," he'd seen pictures of cowboys on the wall. "Except that they weren't cowboys. They were movie stars. Guys who grew up in Glendale [John Wayne] and Santa Monica [Robert Redford]." Surely this desert had its own heroes once, in the old gold-mining towns where a few people still hang on, towns like Goldfield and Tonopah. Remembering those actual heroes would be "culture." Needing pictures of move stars for want of the real thing is only a nostalgia for culture.

Nostalgia is not memory. Memory is specific. One has a relationship to a memory, and it may be a difficult relationship, because a memory always makes a demand upon the present. But nostalgia is vague, a sentimental wash that obscures memory and acts as a narcotic to dull the importance of the present.

Media as we know it now thrives on nostalgia and is hostile to memory. In a television bio-pic, Helen Keller is impersonated by Mare Winningham. But the face of Helen Keller was marked by her enormous powers of concentration, while the face of Mare Winningham is merely cameo-pretty. A memory has been stolen. It takes a beauty in you to see the beauty in Helen Keller's face, while to cast the face of a Mare Winningham in the role is to suggest, powerfully, that one can come back from the depths unscathed. No small delusion is being sold here. Yet this is a minor instance in a worldwide, twenty-four-hour-a-day onslaught.

An onslaught that gathers momentum every twenty-four hours. Remember that what drew us to Las Vegas was a computer fair. One of these new computers does interesting things with photographs. You can put a photograph into the computer digitally. This means the photograph is in there without a negative or print, each element of the image stored separately. In the computer, you can change any element of the photograph you wish, replacing it or combining it with elements from other photographs. In other words, you can take composites of different photographs and put them into a new photograph of your own composition. Combine this with computer drawing, and you can touch up shadows that don't match. When it comes out of the computer the finished product bears no evidence of tampering with[1] any negative. The possibilities for history books and news stories are infinite. Whole new histories can now be written. Events which never happened can be fully documented.

The neo-Nazis who are trying to convince people that the Holocaust never happened will be able to show the readers of their newsletter an Auschwitz of well-fed, happy people being watched over by kindly S.S. men while tending gardens. And they will be able to make the accusation[2] that photographs of the *real* Auschwitz were created in a computer by manipulative Jews. The Soviet Union can rewrite Czechoslovakia and Afghanistan, the United States can rewrite Vietnam, and atomic weapons proponents can prove that the average resident of Hiroshima was unharmed by the blast. On a less sinister, but equally disruptive, level, the writers of business prospectuses and real-estate brochures can have a field day.

Needless to say, when any photograph can be processed this way then all photographs become suspect. It not only becomes easier to lie, it becomes far harder to tell the truth.

But why should this seem shocking when under the names of "entertainment" and "advertising" we've been filming history, and every facet of daily life, in just this way for nearly a century now? It shouldn't surprise us that the ethics of our entertainment have taken over, and that we are viewing reality itself as a form of entertainment. And, as entertainment, reality can be rewritten, transformed, played with, in any fashion.

These considerations place us squarely at the center of our world—and we have no choice, it's the only world there is anymore. *Electronic media has done for everyday reality what*

---

1. If someone tampers with something, they interfere with it or try to change it when they have no right to do so.
2. If you make an accusation against someone, you criticize them or express the belief that they have done something wrong. • Kim rejects accusations that Country music is over-sentimental.

Einstein did for physics: everything is shifting. Even the shifts are shifting. And a fact is not so crucial anymore, not so crucial as the process that turns a fact into an image. For we live now with images as much as facts, and the images seem to impart more life than facts *precisely because they are so capable of transmutation, of transcendence, able to transcend their sources and their uses.* And all the while the images goad us on, so that we become partly images ourselves, imitating the properties of images as we surround ourselves with images.

This is most blatant in our idea of "a vacation"—an idea only about 100 years old. To "vacation" is to enter an image. Las Vegas is only the most shrill embodiment of this phenomenon. People come here not so much to gamble (individual losses are comparatively light), nor for the glittery entertainment, but to step into an image, a daydream, a filmlike world where "everything" is promised. No matter that the Vegas definition of "everything" is severely limited, what thrills tourists is the sense of being surrounded in "real life" by the same images that they see on TV. But the same is true of the Grand Canyon, or Yellowstone National Park, or Yosemite, or Death Valley, or virtually any of our "natural" attractions. What with all their roads, telephones, bars, cable-TV motels, the visitors are carefully protected from having to *experience* the place. They view its image, they camp out in its image, ski down or climb up its image, take deep breaths of its image, let its image give them a tan. Or, when they tour the cities, they ride the quaint trolley cars of the city's image, they visit the Latin Quarter of its image, they walk across the Brooklyn Bridge of its image—our recreation is a *re*-creation of America into one big Disneyland.

And this is only one way we have stripped the very face of America of any content, any reality, concentrating only on its power as image. We also elect images, groom ourselves as images, make an image of our home, our car, and now, with aerobics, of our very bodies. For in the aerobics craze the flesh becomes a garment, susceptible to fashion. So it becomes less *our* flesh, though the exercise may make it more serviceable. It becomes "my" body, like "my" car, "my" house. What, within us, is saying "my"? What is transforming body into image? We shy away from[1] asking. In this sense it can be said that after the age of about twenty-five we no longer *have* bodies anymore—we have possessions that are either more or less young, which we are constantly trying to transform and through which we try to breathe.

I' not that all this transformation of realities into un- or non- or supra-realities is "bad," but that it's unconscious, compulsive, reductive. We rarely make things more than they were; we simplify them into less. Though surely the process *could*—at least theoretically—go both ways. Or so India's meditators and Zen's monks say. But that would be to increase meaning, and we seem bent on the elimination of meaning. We're Reagan's Rangers, climbing a cliff that *is* a real cliff, except it's not the cliff we say it is, so that the meaning of both cliffs—not to mention of our act of climbing—is reduced.

As I look out onto a glowing city that is more than 400 years old but was built only during the last forty years, as I watch it shine in blinking neon in a desert that has seen the flash of atom bombs, it becomes more and more plain to me that America is at war with meaning. America is form opposed to content. Not just form *instead* of content. Form opposed. Often violently. There are few things resented so much among us as the suggestion that what we do *means*. It *means* something to watch so much TV. It means something to be obsessed with sports. It means something to vacation by indulging in images. It means something, and therefore it has consequences. Other cultures have argued over their meanings. We tend to deny that there is any such thing, insisting instead that what you see is what you get and that's *it*. All we're doing is having a *good time*, all we're doing is making a buck, all we're doing is enjoying the spectacle, we insist. So that when we export American culture what we are really exporting is an attitude toward content. Media is the American war on content with all the stops out, with meaning in utter rout, frightened nuances dropping their weapons as they run.

"Media is the history that forgives," my friend Dave Johnson

---

1. If you shy away from doing something, you avoid doing it, often because you are afraid or not confident enough.

told me on a drive through that same desert a few months later. We love to take a weekend every now and again and just *drive.* Maybe it started with reading *On the Road* when we were kids, or watching a great old TV show called *Route 66* about two guys who drove from town to town working at odd jobs and having adventures with intense women who, when asked who they were, might say (as one did), "Suppose I said I was the Queen of Spain?" Or maybe it was all those rock 'n' roll songs about "the road"—the road, where we can blast our tape-decks as loud as we want, and watch the world go by without having to touch it, a trip through the greatest hologram[1] there is, feeling like neither boys nor men but both and something more, embodiments of some ageless, restless principle of movement rooted deep in our prehistory. All of which is to say that we're just as stuck with[2] the compulsion to enter the image as anybody, and that we love the luxuries of fossil fuel just as much as any other red-blooded, thickheaded Americans.

Those drives are our favorite time to talk, and, again, America is our oldest flame. We never tire of speaking of her, nor of our other old girlfriends. For miles and miles of desert I thought of what Dave had said.

"Media is the history that forgives." A lovely way to put it, and quite un-Western. We Westerners tend to think in sets of opposites: good/bad, right/wrong, me/you, past/present. These sets are often either antagonistic (East/West, commie/capitalist, Christian/heathen) or they set up a duality that instantly calls out to be bridged (man/ woman). But Dave's comment sidesteps the dualities and suggests something more complex: a lyrical impulse is alive somewhere in all this media obfuscation. It is the impulse to redeem the past—in his word, to forgive history—by presenting it as we would have most liked it to be.

It is one thing to accuse the media of lying. They are, and they know it, and they know we know, and we know they know that we know, and nothing changes. It is another to recognize

1. A hologram is a three-dimensional photographic image created by laser beams.
2.. If you are stuck with something that you do not want, you cannot get rid of it.
  • Many people are now stuck with expensive fixed-rate mortgages.

the rampant lying shallowness of our media as a massive united longing for ... innocence? For a sheltered childlike state in which we need not know about our world or our past. We are so desperate for this that we are willing to accept ignorance as a substitute for innocence. For there can be no doubt anymore that this society *knowingly* accepts its ignorance as innocence—we have seen so much in the last twenty years that now we know what we *don't* see. Whenever a TV show or a movie or a news broadcast leaves out crucial realities for the sake of sentimentality, we pretty much understand the nature of what's been left out and why.

But American media forgives the emptiness and injustice of our daily life by presenting our daily life as innocent. Society, in turn, forgives American media for lying because if we accept the lie as truth then we needn't do anything, we needn't change.

I like Dave's line of thought because it suggests a motive—literally, a motive force—for these rivers of glop that stream from the screens and loudspeakers of our era. Because, contrary to popular belief, profit is *not* the motive. That seems a rash statement to make in the vicinity of Las Vegas, but the profit motive merely begs the question: why is it profitable? Profit, in media, is simply a way of measuring attention. Why does what we call "media" attract so much attention?

The answer is that it is otherwise too crippling for individuals to bear the strain of accepting the unbalanced, unrewarding, uninspiring existence that is advertised as "normal daily life" for most people who have to earn a living every day.

Do those words seem too strong? Consider: to go to a job you don't value in itself but for its paycheck, while your kids go to a school that is less and less able to educate them; a large percentage of your pay is taken by the government for defenses that don't defend, welfare that doesn't aid, and the upkeep of a government that is impermeable to the influence of a single individual; while you are caught in a value system that judges you by what you own, in a society where it is taken for granted now that children can't communicate with their parents, that old people have to be shut away in homes, and that no neighborhood is *really* safe; while the highest medical costs in the world don't prevent us from having one of the worst health records in the

West (for instance, New York has a far higher infant mortality rate than Hong Kong), and the air, water, and supermarket food are filled with God-knows-what; and to have, at the end of a busy yet uneventful life, little to show for enduring all this but a comfortable home if you've "done well" enough; yet to *know* all along that you're living in the freest, most powerful country in the world, though you haven't had time to exercise much freedom and don't personally have any power—this is to be living a life of slow attrition and maddening contradictions.

Add to this a social style that values cheerfulness more than any other attribute, and then it is not so strange or shocking that the average American family watches six to eight hours of network television a day. It is a cheap and sanctioned way to partake of this world without having actually to live in it.

Certainly they don't watch so much TV because they're bored—there's far too much tension in their lives to call them bored, and, in fact, many of the products advertised on their favorite programs feature drugs to calm them down. Nor is it because they're stupid—a people managing the most technically intricate daily life in history can hardly be written off[1] as stupid; nor because they can't entertain themselves—they are not so different from the hundreds of generations of their forebears who entertained themselves very well as a matter of course. No, they are glued to the TV because one of the most fundamental messages of television is: "It's all right."

Every sitcom and drama says: "It's all right." Those people on the tube go through the same—if highly stylized—frustrations, and are exposed to the same dangers as we are, yet they reappear magically every week (every day on the soap operas) ready for more, always hopeful, always cheery, never questioning the fundamental premise that this is the way a great culture behaves and that all the harassments are the temporary inconveniences of a beneficent society. It's going to get even *better*, but even now *it's all right*. The commercials, the Hollywood movies, the universal demand in every television drama or comedy that no character's hope can ever be exhausted, combine in a deafening chorus of:

---

1. If you write someone or something off, you decide that they are unimportant or useless and that they are not worth further serious attention (=dismiss)

It's all right.

As a screenwriter I have been in many a film production meeting, and not once have I heard any producer or studio executive say, "We have to lie to the public." What I have heard, over and over, is, "They have to leave the theater feeling good." This, of course, easily (though not always) translates into lying—into simplifying emotions and events so that "it's all right." You may measure how deeply our people know "it" is not all right, not at all, by how much money they are willing to pay to be ceaselessly told that it is. The more they feel it's not, the more they need to be told it is—hence Mr. Reagan's popularity.

Works that don't say "It's all right" don't get much media attention or make much money.

The culture itself is in the infantile position of needing to be assured, every day, all day, that this way of life is good for you. Even the most disturbing news is dispensed[1] in the most reassuring package. As world news has gotten more and more disturbing, the trend in broadcast journalism has been to get more and more flimflam, to take it less seriously, to keep up the front of "It's really quite all right. This creates an enormous tension between the medium and its messages, because everybody knows that what's on the news is *not* all right. That is why such big money is paid to a newscaster with a clam, authoritative air who, by his presence alone, seems to resolve the contradictions of his medium. Walter Cronkite was the most popular newscaster in broadcast history because his very presence implied: "As long as I'm on the air, you can be sure that, no matter what I'm telling you, *it's still all right.*"

Which is to say that the media has found it profitable to do the mothering of the mass psyche. But it's a weak mother. It cannot nurture. All it can do is say it's all right, tuck us in, and hope for the best.

Today most serous, creative people exhaust themselves in a sideline commentary on this state of affairs, a commentary that usually gets sucked up into the media and spewed back out in a format that says ""It's all fight. What this guy's saying is quite

1. If someone dispenses something that they own or control, they give or provide it to a number of people.

all right, what this woman's singing is all right, all right." This is what "gaining recognition" virtually always means now in America: your work gets turned inside out so that its meaning becomes "It's all right."

Of course, most of what exist to *make media of*, to make images of, is more and more disorder. Media keeps saying, "It's all right" while being fixated upon the violent, the chaotic, and the terrifying. So the production of media becomes more and more schizoid, with two messages simultaneously being broadcast: "It's all right, We're dying. It's all right. We're all dying." The other crucial message — "We're dying" — runs right alongside *It's all right*.

Murder is the crux of much media "drama" But it's murder presented harmlessly, with trivial causes cited[1], Rare is the attempt, in all our thousands of murder dramas, to delve below the surface. We take for granted now, almost as an immutable principle of dramatic unity, that significant numbers of us want to kill significant numbers of the rest of us. And what are all the murders in our media but a way of saying "We are being killed, we are killing, we are dying"? Only a people dying and in the midst of death would need to see so much of it in such sanitized form *in order to make death harmless*. This is the way we choose to share our death.

Delete the word " entertainment" and say instead, North Americans devote an enormous amount of time to the ritual of sharing death. If this were recognized as a ritual, and if the deaths were shared with a respect for the realities and the mysteries of death, this might be a very useful thing to do. But there is no respect for death in our death-dependent media, there is only the compulsion to display death. As for the consumers, they consume these deaths like sugar pills. Their ritual goes on far beneath any level on which they'd be prepared to admit the word "ritual." So we engage in a ritual we pretend isn't happening, hovering around deaths that we say aren't real.

It is no coincidence that this practice has thrived while the Pentagon uses the money of these death watchers to create

1. If you cite something, you quote it or mention it, especially as an example or proof of what you are saying.

weapons for death on a scale that is beyond the powers of human imagination — the very same human imagination that is stunting itself by watching ersatz[1] deaths, as though intentionally crippling its capacity to envision the encroaching dangers. It is possible that the Pentagon's process could not go on without the dulling effects of this "entertainment."

When we're not watching our screens, we're listening to music. And, of course, North Americans listen to love songs at every possible opportunity, through every possible orifice[2] of media. People under the strain of such dislocating unrealities need to hear "I love you, I love you," as often as they can. "I love you" or "I used to love you" or "I ought to love you" or "I need to love you" or "I want to love you." It is the fashion of pop-music critics to discount the words for the style, forgetting that most of the world's cultures have had songs about *everything*, songs about work, about the sky, about death, about the gods, about getting up in the morning, about animals, about children, about eating, about dreams—about everything, along with love. These were songs that everybody knew and sang. For a short time in the late sixties we moved toward such songs again, but that was a brief digression; since the First World War the music that most North Americans listen to has been a music of love lyrics that rarely go beyond adolescent yearnings. Either the song is steeped in the yearnings themselves, or it is saturated with a longing for the days when one could, shamelessly, feel like an adolescent. The beat has changed radically from decade to decade, but with brief exceptions that beat has carried the same pathetic load. (The beat, thankfully, has given us other gifts.)

It can't be over-emphasized that these are entertainments of a people whose basic imperative is the need not to think about their *environment*. The depth of their need may be measured by the hysterical popularity of this entertainment; it is also the measure of how little good it does them.

Media is not experience. In its most common form, media

1. If you describe something as ersatz, you dislike it because it is not genuine and is a poor imitation of something better. (=fake)
2. An orifice is an opening or hole, especially one in your body such as your mouth.

substitutes a fantasy of experience or (in the case of news) an abbreviation of experience for the living fact. But in our culture the absorption of media has become a substitute for experience. We absorb media, we don't live it—there is a vast psychological difference, and it is a difference that is rarely brought up.

For example, in the 1940, when one's environment was still one's environment, an experience to be lived instead of a media-saturation to be absorbed, teenagers like Elvis Presley and Jerry Lee Lewis didn't learn their music primarily from the radio. Beginning when they were small boys they sneaked over to the black juke joints of Louisiana and Mississippi and Tennessee, where they weren't supposed to go, and they listened and learned. When Lewis and Presley began recording, even though they were barely twenty they had tremendous authority because they had experience—a raw experience of crossing foreign boundaries, of streets and sounds and peoples, of the night-to-night learning of ways that could not be taught at home.

This is very different from young musicians now who learn from a product, not a living ground. Their music doesn't get to them till it's been sifted through elaborate corporate networks of production and distribution. It doesn't smack of the raw world that exists before "product" can even be thought of.

The young know this, of course. They sense the difference intensely, and often react to it violently. So white kids from suburban media culture invented slam dancing (jumping up and down and slamming into each other) while black kids from the South Bronx, who have to deal with realities far more urgent than media, were elaborating the astounding graces of break dancing.

Slam dancing was a dead end. Break dancing, coming from a living ground, goes out through media but becomes ultimately transformed into another living ground—the kids in the elementary school down the street in Santa Monica break dance. Which is to say, a grace has been added to their lives. A possibility of grace. With the vitality that comes from having originated from a living ground. The media here is taking its proper role as a channel, not as a world in itself. It's possible that these kids are being affected more in their bodies and their daily lives by the South Bronx subculture than by high-gloss films like

Gremlins or *Indiana Jones and the Temple of Doom*. Even through all this static, life can speak to life.

Of course, break dancing inevitably gets hyped, and hence devalued, by the entertainment industry, the way Elvis Presley ended up singing "Viva Las Vegas" as that town's most glamorous headliner. He went from being the numinous son of a living ground to being the charismatic product of a media empire—the paradigm of media's power to transform the transformers. The town veritably glows in the dark with the strength of media's mystique.

We do not yet know what life is in a media environment. We have not yet evolved a contemporary culture that can supply the definition—or rather, supply the constellation of concepts in which that definition would live and grow. These seem such simple statements, but they are at the crux of the American dilemma now. An important aspect of this dilemma is that we've barely begun a body of thought and art which is focused on what is really alive in the ground of a media-saturated daily life. For culture always proceeds from two poles: one is the people of the land and the street; the other is the thinker. You see this most starkly in revolutions: the ground swell[1] on the one hand, the thinker (the Jefferson, for instance) on the other. Or religiously, the ground swell of belief that is articulated by a Michelangelo or a Dante. The two poles can exist without each other but they cannot be effective without each other.

Unless a body of thought connects with a living ground, there is no possibility that this era will discover itself within its cacophony and create, one day, a post-A.D. culture. It is ours to attempt the thought and seek the ground—for all of us exist between those poles. We are not only dying. We are living. And we are struggling to share our lives, which is all, finally, that "culture" means.

1. A sudden growth of public feeling or support for something is often called a ground swell.

AFTER YOU READ

1. Now what is the environment of America?

2. Who first use the word El Dorado?

3. The writer says, "Nostalgia is not memory." How does he define nostalgia?

4. When any photograph can be processed this way, all photographs become suspect. Why should this seem shocking, when under the names of "entertainment and advertising"?

5. The writer says, "To 'vacation' is to enter an image." Which city shows the image best?

6. How does American media forgives the emptiness and injustice of our daily life?

7. Why does a medium give big money to a newscaster?

8. Pentagon's process could not go on without these. What are these?

9. On what condition will the era discover itself within its cacophony and create, one day, a post-A.D. culture?

7

J.K. ROWLING: HARVARD COMMENCEMENT SPEECH 2008

by J. K. Rowling

The Fringe Benefits[1] of Failure, and the Importance of Imagination

President Faust, members of the Harvard Corporation and the Board of Overseers, members of the faculty, proud parents, and above all, graduates.

The first thing I would like to say is 'thank you.' Not only has Harvard given me an extraordinary honour, but the weeks of fear and nausea[2] I have endured at the thought of giving this commencement address have made me lose weight. A win-win situation! Now all I have to do is take deep breaths, squint[3] at the red banners and convince myself that I am at the world's largest Gryffindor[4] reunion.

Delivering a commencement address is a great responsibility; or so I thought until I cast my mind back to[5] my own graduation. The commencement speaker that day was the distinguished British philosopher Baroness Mary Warnock. Reflecting on her

1. Fringe Benefits are extra things that some people get from their job in addition to their salary, for example a car.
2. Nausea is the condition of feeling that you are going to vomit. I was overcome with a feeling of nausea
3. If you squint at something, you look at it with your eyes partly closed.
4. Gryffindor values courage, bravery, daring, nerve and chivalry
5. If you cast your mind back to a time in the past, you think about what happened then. • Cast your mind back to 1978, when Forest won the title.

speech has helped me enormously in writing this one, because it turns out that I can't remember a single word she said. This liberating discovery enables me to proceed without any fear that I might inadvertently influence you to abandon promising careers in business, the law or politics for the giddy[1] delights of becoming a gay wizard.

You see? If all you remember in years to come is the 'gay wizard' joke, I've come out ahead of Baroness Mary Warnock. Achievable goals: the first step to self improvement.

Actually, I have wracked[2] my mind and heart for what I ought to say to you today. I have asked myself what I wish I had known at my own graduation, and what important lessons I have learned in the 21 years that have expired between that day and this.

I have come up with two answers. On this wonderful day when we are gathered together to celebrate your academic success, I have decided to talk to you about the benefits of failure. And as you stand on the threshold of what is sometimes called 'real life', I want to extol[3] the crucial importance of imagination.

These may seem quixotic or paradoxical choices, but please bear with me[4].

Looking back at the 21-year-old that I was at graduation, is a slightly uncomfortable experience for the 42-year-old that she has become. Half my lifetime ago I was striking an uneasy balance[5] between the ambition I had for myself, and what those closest to me expected of me.

---

1. If you feel giddy, you feel unsteady and think that you are about to fall over, usually because you are not well. • He felt giddy and light-headed.(=dizzy)
2. wrack: 고문하다, 괴롭히다.
3. If you extol something or someone, you praise them enthusiastically. • Now experts are extolling the virtues.
4. If you ask someone to bear with you, you are asking them to be patient. • If you'll bear with me, Frank, just let me try to explain.
5. strike a balance : 공평한 해결을 찾아내다

I was convinced that the only thing I wanted to do, ever, was to write novels. However, my parents, both of whom came from impoverished background and neither of whom had been to college, took the view that my overactive imagination was an amusing personal quirk that would never pay a mortgage, or secure a pension. I know that the irony strikes with the force of a cartoon anvil[1], now.

So they hoped that I would take a vocational degree; I wanted to study English Literature. A compromise was reached that in retrospect satisfied nobody, and I went up to study Modern Languages. Hardly had my parents' car rounded the corner at the end of road than I ditched[2] German and scuttled off down the Classics corridor.

I cannot remember telling my parents that I was studying Classic; they might well have found out for the first time on graduation day. Of all the subjects on this planet, I think they would have been hard put to[3] name one less useful than Greek mythology when it came to securing the keys to an executive bathroom.

I would like to make it clear, in parenthesis[4], that I do not blame my parents for their point of view. There is an expiry date on blaming your parents for steering you in the wrong direction; the moment you are old enough to take the wheel, responsibility lies with you. What is more, I cannot criticise my parents for hoping that I would never experience poverty. They had been poor themselves, and I have since been poor, and I quite agree

1. Anvil cartoons from the cartoon stock Directory - the world's largest on-line collection of cartoons.
2. If you ditch something that you have or are responsible, you abandon it or get rid of it, because you no longer want it.
   *I decided to ditch the sofa bed.(=dump)
3. If someone is hard put to do something or, in British English if they are hard pushed to do something, they have great difficulty doing it.
   *Mr. Morton is undoubtedly cleverer than Mr. Kirby, but he will be hard put to match his popularity.
4. You say in parenthesis to indicate that you are about to add something before going back to the main topic. 덧붙여서

with them that it is not an ennobling experience. Poverty entails fear, and stress, and sometimes depression; it means a thousand petty humiliations and hardships. Climbing out of poverty by your own efforts, that is indeed something on which to pride yourself, but poverty itself is romanticised only by fools.

What I feared most for myself at your age was not poverty, but failure.

At your age, in spite of a distinct lack of motivation at university, where I had spent far too long in the coffee bar writing stories, and far too little time at lectures, I had a knack[1] for passing examinations, and that, for years, had been the measure of success in my life and that of my peers.

I am not dull enough to suppose that because you are young, gifted and well-educated, you have never known hardship or heartbreak. Talent and intelligence never yet inoculated anyone against the caprice of the Fates, and I do not for a moment suppose that everyone here has enjoyed an existence of unruffled[2] privilege and contentment.

However, the fact that you are graduating from Harvard suggests that you are not very well-acquainted with failure. You might be driven by a fear of failure quite as much as a desire for success. Indeed, your conception of failure might not be too far from the average person's idea of success, so high have you already flown.

Ultimately, we all have to decide for ourselves what constitutes failure, but the world is quite eager to give you a set of criteria if you let it. So I think it fair to say that by any conventional measure, a mere seven years after my graduation day, I had failed on an epic scale. An exceptionally short-lived marriage had

---

1. A knack is a particularly clever or skillful way of doing something successfully, especially something which most people find difficult.
2. If you describe someone as unruffled, you mean that they are calm and do not seem to be affected by surprising or frightening events.(=unperturbed)

imploded[1], and I was jobless, a lone parent, and as poor as it is possible to be in modern Britain, without being homeless. The fears that my parents had had for me, and that I had had for myself, had both come to pass, and by every usual standard, I was the biggest failure I knew.

Now, I am not going to stand here and tell you that failure is fun. That period of my life was a dark one, and I had no idea that there was going to be what the press has since represented as a kind of fairy tale resolution. I had no idea then how far the tunnel extended, and for a long time, any light at the end of it was a hope rather than a reality.

So why do I talk about the benefits of failure? Simply because failure meant a stripping away[2] of the inessential. I stopped pretending to myself that I was anything other than what I was, and began to direct all my energy into finishing the only work that mattered to me. Had I really succeeded at anything else, I might never have found the determination to succeed in the one arena I believed I truly belonged. I was set free, because my greatest fear had been realised, and I was still alive, and I still had a daughter whom I adored, and I had an old typewriter and a big idea. And so rock bottom became the solid foundation on which I rebuilt my life.

You might never fail on the scale I did, but some failure in life is inevitable. It is impossible to live without failing at something, unless you live so cautiously that you might as well not have lived at all—in which case, you fail by default.

Failure gave me an inner security that I had never attained by passing examinations. Failure taught me things about myself that I could have learned no other way. I discovered that I had a strong will, and more discipline than I had suspected; I also found out that I had friends whose value was truly above the price of

1. If something implodes, it collapses into itself in a sudden and violent way.
2. To strip away something, especially something that hides the true nature of a thing, means to remove it completely.

rubies.

The knowledge that you have emerged wiser and stronger from setbacks means that you are, ever after, secure in your ability to survive. You will never truly know yourself, or the strength of your relationships, until both have been tested by adversity. Such knowledge is a true gift, for all that it is painfully won, and it has been worth more than any qualification I ever earned.

So given a Time Turner, I would tell my 21-year-old self that personal happiness lies in knowing that life is not a check-list of acquisition or achievement. Your qualifications, your CV[1], are not your life, though you will meet many people of my age and older who confuse the two. Life is difficult, and complicated, and beyond anyone's total control, and the humility to know that will enable you to survive its vicissitudes[2].

Now you might think that I chose my second theme, the importance of imagination, because of the part it played in rebuilding my life, but that is not wholly so. Though I personally will defend the value of bedtime stories to my last gasp, I have learned to value imagination in a much broader sense. Imagination is not only the uniquely human capacity to envision that which is not, and therefore the fount[3] of all invention and innovation. In its arguably most transformative and revelatory capacity, it is the power that enables us to empathise with[4] humans whose experiences we have never shared.

One of the greatest formative experiences of my life preceded Harry Potter, though it informed much of what I subsequently

---

1. Curriculum Vitae
2. You use vicissitudes to refer to changes, especially unpleasant ones, that happen to someone or something at difficult times in their life or development.
   *Whatever the vicissitudes of her past life, Jill now seems to have come through.
3. If you describe a person or thing as the fount of something, you are saying that they are an important source or supply of it.
   *To the young boy his father was the fount of all knowledge.
4. If you empathize with someone, you understand their situation, problems and feelings because you have been in a similar situation.

wrote in those books. This revelation came in the form of one of my earliest day jobs.

Though I was sloping off[1] to write stories during my lunch hours, I paid the rent in my early 20s by working at the Africa research department at Amnesty International's headquarters in London.

There in my little office I read hastily scribbled letters smuggled out of totalitarian regimes by men and women who were risking imprisonment to inform the outside world of what was happening to them. I saw photographs of those who had disappeared without trace, sent to Amnesty by their desperate families and friends. I read the testimony of torture victims and saw pictures of their injuries. I opened handwritten, eye-witness accounts of summary trials and executions, of kidnappings and rapes.

Many of my co-workers were ex-political prisoners, people who had been displaced from their homes, or fled into exile, because they had the temerity[2] to speak against their governments. Visitors to our offices included those who had come to give information, or to try and find out what had happened to those they had left behind.

I shall never forget the African torture victim, a young man no older than I was at the time, who had become mentally ill after all he had endured in his homeland. He trembled uncontrollably as he spoke into a video camera about the brutality inflicted upon him. He was a foot taller than I was, and seemed as fragile as a child. I was given the job of escorting him back to the Underground Station afterwards, and this man whose life had been shattered by cruelty took my hand with exquisite courtesy, and wished me future happiness.

1. If you slope off, you go away quickly and quietly as if you are trying to escape or avoid something(=slink off)
2. If you say that a person has the temerity to do something, you are annoyed about something they have done which you think showed a respect.

And as long as I live I shall remember walking along an empty corridor and suddenly hearing, from behind a close door, a scream of pain and horror such as I have never heard since. The door opened, and the researcher poked out her head and told me to run and make a hot drink for the young man sitting with her. She had just had to give him the news that in retaliation for his own outspokenness against his country's regime, his mother had been seized and executed.

Every day of my working week in my early 20s I was reminded how incredibly fortunate I was, to live in a country with a democratically elected government, where legal representation and public trial were the rights of everyone.

Every day, I saw more evidence about the evils humankind will inflict on their fellow humans, to gain or maintain power. I began to have nightmares, literal nightmares, about some of the things I saw, heard, and read.

And yet I also learned more about human goodness at Amnesty International than I had ever known before.

Amnesty mobilises thousands of people who have never been tortured or imprisoned for their beliefs to act on behalf of those who have. The power of human empathy, leading to collective action, saves lives, and frees prisoners. Ordinary people, whose personal well-being and security are assured, join together in huge numbers to save people they do not know, and will never meet. My small participation in that process was one of the most humbling and inspiring experiences of my life.

Unlike any other creature on this planet, human can learn and understand, without having experienced. They can think themselves into other people's places.

Of course, this is a power, like my brand of fictional magic, that is morally neutral. One might use such an ability to manipulate, or control, just as much as to understand or sympathise.

And many prefer not to exercise their imaginations at all. They choose to remain comfortably within the bounds of their own experience, never troubling to wonder how it would feel to have been born other than they are. They can refuse to hear screams or to peer inside cages; they can close their minds and hearts to any suffering that does not touch them personally; they can refuse to know.

I might be tempted to envy people who can live that way, except that I do not think they have any fewer nightmares than I do. Choosing to live in narrow spaces leads to a form of mental agoraphobia[1], and that brings its own terrors. I think the wilfully unimaginative see more monsters. They are often more afraid.

What is more, those who choose not to empathise enable real monsters. For without ever committing an act of outright evil ourselves, we collude[2] with it, through our own apathy.

One of many things I learned at the end of that Classics corridor down which I ventured at the age of 18, in search of something I could not then define, was this, written by the Greek author Plutarch: what we achieve inwardly will change our reality.

That is an astonishing statement and yet proven a thousand times every day of our lives. It expresses, in part, our inescapable connection with the outside world, the fact that we touch other people's lives simply by existing.

But how much more are you, Harvard graduates of 2008, likely to touch other people's lives? Your intelligence, your capacity for hard work, the education you have earned and received, give you unique status, and unique responsibilities. Even your nationality sets you apart. The great majority of you belong to the world's only remaining superpower. The way you vote, the

1. Agoraphobia is the fear of open or public places.
2. If one person collude with another, they co-operate with them secretly or illegally.
   • Several local officials are in jail on charge of colluding with the Mafia.

way you live, the way you protest, the pressure you bring to bear on your government, has an impact way beyond your borders. That is your privilege, and your burden.

If you choose to use your status and influence to raise your voice on behalf of those who have no voice; if you choose to identify not only with the powerful, but with the powerless; if you retain the ability to imagine yourself into the lives of those who do not have your advantages, then it will not only be your proud families who celebrate your existence, but thousands and millions of people whose reality you have helped change. We do not need magic to change the world, we carry all the power we need inside ourselves already: we have the power to imagine better.

I am nearly finished. I have one last hope for you, which is something that I already had at 21. The friends with whom I sat on graduation day have been my friends for life. They are my children's godparents, the people to whom I've been able to turn in times of trouble, people who have been kind enough not to sue me when I took their names for Death Eaters. At our graduation we were bound by enormous affection, by our shared experience of a time that could never come again, and, of course, by the knowledge that we held certain photographic evidence that would be exceptionally valuable if any of us ran for Prime Minister.

So today, I wish you nothing better than similar friendships. And tomorrow, I hope that even if you remember not a single word of mine, you remember those of Seneca, another of those old Romans I met when I fled down the Classics corridor, in retreat from career ladders, in search of ancient wisdom:

As is a tale, so is life: not how long it is, but how good it is, is what matters.

I wish you all very good lives.

Thank you very much.

AFTER YOU READ

1. What is J.K Rowling's major?

2. What was the only thing she wanted to do ever?

3. What makes her think that process one of the most humbling and inspiring experiences of her life?

4. What does she define imagination?

5. What kind of thing did she discover through failure?

6. What became the solid foundation on which she built her life?

7. What did her parents hope that she would study?

8

CHIEF SEATTLE'S LETTER TO ALL

<Chief Seattle, Chief of the Suquamish Indians wrote to the American Government in the 1800's. In his letter he gave the most profound understanding of God in all things. Here is his letter, which should be instilled in the hearts and minds of every parent and child in all the Nations of the World.>

The Great Chief in Washington sends word that he wishes to buy our land. The Great Chief also sends us words of friendship and goodwill. This is kind of him, since we know he has little need of our friendship in return. But we will consider your offer, for we know that if we do not sell, the whiteman may come with guns and take our land.

How can you buy or sell the sky, the warmth of the land? The idea is strange to us. If we do not own the freshness of the air and the sparkle of the water, how can you buy them? Every part of this earth is sacred to my people—every shining pine needle, every sandy shore, every mist in the dark woods, every clearing and humming insect is holy in the memory and experience of my people. The sap which courses through the trees carries the memories of the redman. The whiteman's dead forget the country of their birth when they go to walk among the stars. Our dead nerver forget this beautiful earth, for it is the mother of the redman: we are part of the earth and it is part of us. The perfumed flowers are our sisters; the bear, the deer, the great eagle, these are our brothers. The rocky crests, the dew in the meadows, the body heat of the pony and man all belong to the same family.

So when the Great Chief in Washington sends word that he wishes to buy our land, he asks much of us. The Great Chief sends word that he will reserve us a place so that we can live comfortably, to ourselves. He will be our father and we will be his children. So we will consider your offer to buy our land, but it will not be easy, for this land is sacred to us. This shining water that moves in the streams and rivers is not just water, but the blood of our ancestors. If we sell you our land, you must remember that it is sacred, and you must teach your children that it is sacred, and that each ghostly reflection in the clear water of the lakes tells of events and memories in the life of my people. The water's murmur is the voice of my father's father. The rivers are our brothers, they quench our thirst. The rivers carry our canoes and they feed our children. If we sell you our land you must remember and teach your children that the rivers are our brothers, and yours, and you must henceforth give the rivers the kindness you would give any brother.

The redman has always retreated before the advancing whiteman, as the mist of the mountains runs before the morning sun, but the ashes of our fathers are sacred, their graves are holy ground. And so these hills, these trees, this portion of the earth is consecrated to us. We know that the whiteman does not understand our ways—one portion of sand is the same to him as the next, for he is a stranger who comes in the night and takes what he needs. The earth is not his brother but his enemy, and when he has conquered it he moves on. He leaves his fathers' graves behind and he does not care; he kidnaps the earth from his children, he does not care. His fathers' graves and his childrens' birthrights are forgotten. He treats his mother the earth and his brother the sky as things to be bought, plundered, sold like sheep or bright beads. His appetite will devour the earth and leave behind only a desert.

I do not know; our ways are different from your ways. The sight of your cities pains the eyes of the redman, but perhaps it is because the redman is a savage and does not understand. There is no quiet place in the whiteman's cities—no place to hear the unfurling of leaves in spring or the rustle of insects' wings. But perhaps it is because I am a savage and do not understand. The clatter only seems to insult the ears. And what is there to life if a man cannot hear the lonely cry of the whippoorwill[1], or the

1 whippoorwill: 북미산 쏙독새

arguments of the frogs round the pond at night? I am a redman and do not understand. The Indian prefers the soft sound of the wind darting over the face of a pond, and the smell of the wind itself, cleansed by a midday rain or scented by the pinyon pine. The air is precious to the redman, for all things share the same breath. The beast, the tree, the man, they all share the same breath. The whiteman does not seem to notice the air he breathes: like a man dying for many days he is numb to the stench.

But if we sell you our land, you must remember that the air is precious to us, that the air shares its spirit with all the life it supports. The wind that gave our grandfather his first breath also receives his last sigh. The wind must also give our children the spirit of life. And if we sell you our land, you must keep it apart and sacred as a place where even the whitman can go to taste the wind that is sweetened by the meadow's flowers.

So we will consider your offer to buy our land. If we decide to accept, I will make one condition: the whiteman must treat the beasts of this land as his brothers. I am a savage and I do not understand any other way. I have seen a thousand rotting buffaloes on the prairie, left by the whiteman who shot them from a passing train. I am a savage and I do not understand how the smoking iron horse can be more important than the buffalo that we kill only to stay alive. What is man without the beasts? If all the beasts were gone man would die of a great loneliness of spirit, for whatever happens to the beasts soon happens to man. All things are connected.

You must teach your children that the ground beneath their feet is the ashes of our grandfathers. So that they will respect the land, tell your children that the earth is rich with the lives of our kin. Teach your children what we have taught our children—that the earth is our mother. Whatever befalls[1] the earth befalls the sons of the earth; if men spit upon the ground, they spit upon themselves. This we know—the earth does not belong to man, man belongs to the earth. This we know. All things are connected, like the blood which unites one family. All things are connected. Whatever befalls the earth befalls the sons of the earth. Man did not weave the web of life, he is merely a strand in it. Whatever

1. befall: happen to

he does to the web he does to himself.

But we will consider your offer to go to the reservation you have for my people. We will live apart and in peace. It matters little where we spend the rest of our days—our children have seen their fathers humbled in defeat; our warriors have felt shame and after defeat they turn their days in idleness and contaminate their bodies with sweet foods and strong drink. It matters little where we pass the rest of our days. They are not many: a few more hours, a few more winters and none of the children of the great tribes that once lived on this earth, or that roam now in small bands in the woods, will be left to mourn the graves of a people once as powerful and hopeful as yours. But how should I mourn the passing of my people? Tribes are made of men, nothing more. Men come and go like the waves of the sea. Even the whiteman whose God walks and talks with him as friend to friend cannot be exempt from the common destiny. We may be brothers after all, we shall see.

One thing we know, which the whiteman may one day discover—our God is the same God. You may think now that you own Him as you wish to own our land, but you cannot. He is the God of man, and his compassion is equal for the redman and the white. This earth is precious to Him, and to harm the earth is to heap contempt on its Creator. The whites too shall pass, perhaps sooner than other tribes. Continue to contaminate your bed and you will one night suffocate in your own waste. But in your perishing you will shine brightly, fired by the strength of the God who brought you to this land and for some special purpose gave you dominion over this land and over the redman. That destiny is a mystery to us, for we do not understand when the buffalo are all slaughtered, the wild horses are tamed, the secret corners of the forest are heavy with the scent of many men, and the view of the ripe hills is blotted with talking wires. Where will the thicket[1] be? Gone! Where will the eagle be? Gone! And what is it to say goodbye to the swift pony and the hunt? The end of living and the beginning of survival.

So we will consider your offer to buy our land. If we agree it will be to secure the reservation you have promised; there

1. thicket: tangle of shrubs or trees

perhaps we may live out our brief days as we wish. When the last redman has vanished from this earth and his memory is only the shadow of a cloud moving across the prairie, these shores and forests will still hold the spirits of my people. For they love this earth, as the newborn loves its mother's heartbeat. So if we sell you our land, love it as we have loved it; care for it as we have cared for it; hold in your mind the memory of the land as it is when you take it; and with all your strength, with all your heart, preserve it for your children and love it, as God loves us all.

One thing we know: Our God is the same God. This earth is precious to Him. Even the whiteman cannot be exempt from the common destiny. We may be brothers after all—we shall see.

AFTER YOU READ

1. What does the Great Chief think of the earth?

2. Why do the redman's dead never forget this beautiful earth?

3. Why is the air precious to the redman?

4. Why would man die of great loneliness of spirit without the beasts?

5. What does the Great Chief regard the whiteman as?

9

THE ART OF MEDITATION

by Ardis Whitman

A year ago, a family I know sent their 15-year-old daughter to camp with expectations that she would return bearing medals for swimming and horseback riding. Instead, she came back with a new air of quiet and poise[1], and every night retired to her bedroom for half an hour after dinner. Once, when her mother looked in, she found her daughter sitting quietly, hands in her lap, watching the flame of a candle.

What on earth was she doing? "Just meditating," the girl said. It made her feel calmer, she explained, more at peace with herself and the world around her. Lots of people were doing it.

They are, indeed. On a beach in Maine a couple sit, hands folded, oblivious[2] to the screaming of children round about. At a religious festival in Colorado, hundreds of young people hike miles in cold and darkness to meditate on a mountaintop at dawn. Thousands of their elders seem scarcely less interested. Housewives, reformed drug addicts, psychologists, clergymen—all have become unlikely allies in an inward search for understanding.

Many of today's meditators find their inspiration in the great Eastern religions. In fact, it has been estimated that there are a half-million members of various Eastern religious groups in the United States today, and all employ meditative techniques. In addition, there is the "transcendental meditation" of Maharishi Mahesh Yogi, a physicist turned Hindu monk.

1. poise: balance; stability
2. oblivious: forgetful or unmindful

Its practitioners[1](the movement here has grown to nearly 200,000 in five years) meditate twice daily by silently repeating a "mantra[2]"—a Sanskrit sound selected for them by their teachers.

But Eastern techniques are only the most obvious evidence of the new enthusiasm. In Christian churches, too, old methods of meditation have found new popularity. Many church services[3] begin or end with meditation. The youthful Jesus movement[4] practices it, and so does the burgeoning Catholic Pentecostal movement[5]. Religious retreats centering on meditation are also common, and smaller groups often meet in homes.

The art of meditation has deeper roots in our culture than we realize. One dictionary defines meditation as "sustained reflection" and also as "the continuous application of the mind to the contemplation of some religious truth, mystery or object of reverence." The word is also used to describe numerous states of reverie[6] from which new ideas, innovations and even personality changes may spring. In one form or another, such activities are as old and as universal as the human race.

"Meditation has been used in every part of the world and from the remotest periods," wrote Aldous Huxley[7], "as a method for acquiring knowledge about the essential nature of things."

Recently, I sat in a bus beside a young graduate student on his way to a meditation course. "It's the greatest adventure of them all," he said. "You don't know what you're going to find, but whatever it is, you know it's going to change your life." That view is widely accepted. We are in an exploring age. In search of treasure and discovery, we go down to the floor of the sea, scale the highest mountains, even journey toward the stars. With the

---

1. practitioner: one that does something or follow some course or regimen habitually or customarily
2. mantra: a hymn or portion of text, esp. from the Veda, chanted or intoned as an incantation or prayer
3 service: public worship
4. the youthful Jesus movement: 젊은 예수 운동(개신교 선교 단체에서 시행하는 선교 운동임)
5. Catholic Pentecostal movement: 카톨릭교회의 오순절 운동
6. reverie: dreamy thinking or imagining, esp. of agreeable things; fanciful musing; daydreaming
7. Aldous Huxley: (1894~1963) 영국의 소설가이자 비평가로 다방면에 해박한 지식과 번뜩이는 재치로 유명하다.

same intent, we are beginning to travel to the depths of our own consciousness. Today's meditators dream of some great adventure in consciousness, and grope for a new vision that can reshape troubled lives.

How do they do it? A few simple recommendations are almost universal. First, anyone who wants to meditate successfully must set aside a quiet time each day, usually about a half-hour. This must be done consistently, because the results are cumulative and will not appear in a single session. The place you select for meditation also matters. In my own private poll, I found many people who meditate best in an empty church. Perhaps even more often, experienced meditators turn to natural locales—a forest, a lonely shore. Each answers the need to be alone and the need for a feeling of space.

Most important is attitude. All the various techniques of meditation seek to produce a state of openness, inner calm and increased self-awareness. But no one can see into the depth of his mind when it is whirling about like a cyclone. Hence the seemingly absurd devices of posture and concentration—which are designed as aids to quiet the storm of daily concerns.

Apparently they work. A person needn't sit crosslegged on the floor; he might choose, instead, to sit quietly upright in a straight-backed chair. One of the most widely practiced ways to relax the minds is to concentrate on some operation of the body—perhaps the act of breathing.

Meditation is not an escape from daily living, but a preparation for it, and what is of surpassing importance is what we bring back from the experience. Like pearl divers, meditators plunge deep into the inner ocean of consciousness and hope to come swimming back to the surface with jewels of great price. What sorts of jewels? What, in fact, can be found when we look within?

Answers to problems. At the most modest level, by providing a way of staying with an issue long enough to turn all its facets to the light, meditation can help solve day-to-day problems. One man, burdened with a periodically insane wife and three troubled adolescent children, told me that his only cure, when difficulties get too pressing, is to take out his sailboat. Outbound[1], he said, "I don't think about my troubles. I concentrate on the sun on the water; I watch the sails bending in the wind. Sometimes I think about all the other men who have put out to sea, and I wonder what they thought about. By the time I am inbound my mind is calm. Then I begin to see things as they really are, and find I can deal with them."

If meditation accomplishes no more than that, it has done a great deal. A few years ago, psychoanalyst Erich Fromm[2], after addressing a Canadian audience, was asked for "a practical solution to the problems of living." "Quietness," Fromm replied at once. "The experience of stillness. You have to stop in order to be able to change direction."

Self-Discovery. But problem solving is only the kindergarten of meditation. The technique can also be a path to self-discovery. For one thing, you can't sit in concentrated silence for very long without learning something about your physical self. For a child, his body is himself. But somehow, over the years, our minds and bodies divide and become strangers. Meditation can bring them back together, serving one another.

Some trained meditators, in fact, become so attentive to the body and its signals that they can actually teach themselves to control breathing and heartbeat. Even the average person, sitting alone in quiet contemplation, can get a new, sharpened sense of the miracle of his physical being by such artless[3] devices as taking note of the movement of the wind across his face, or feeling muscles move and flex at his behest[4].

In meditation, we also rediscover our memories, the past dreams and experiences which have made us ourselves. If we meditate often enough, inevitably these forgotten details are recovered. "I didn't just remember it, I was there again," one meditator said after an intense session. "I was a child again. I heard the music box playing, sat at the table with my family and tasted the tarts[5] my mother used to make."

---

1. outbound: outward bound
2. Erich Fromm: (1900~80) 독일 태생의 미국의 정신분석학자, 사회철학자
3. artless: without artificiality; simple; natural
4. behest: an order, command, or request
5. tart: a small pie filled with fruit or jam and often having a top crust

One big discovery that everyone makes in meditating is that we have spent our lives changing, and that we will continue to change. "I am trying to decide whether to end my marriage," a correspondent[1] wrote. "We were so happy together once. It took me hours of thinking alone to realize that I am not the same person I was then; and neither is he. Whatever we decide to do, it is two new people who are going to do it."

The way to others. The stream of consciousness that runs through our minds runs through other minds as well, and so we can find much that is universal, much that unite us with others, by looking within. Indeed, many recognize this and meditate together. Without speech, they feel a warm tide of love flowing between them. We experience our likeness, our shared humanity. Indeed we are like torches lit from each other; illumine the one and the other takes fire. A New York psychiatrist once explained it unforgettably to me. "The deeper we go," he said,"the closer we are."

Even solitary meditation helps us understand one another. To put it simply, when we know ourselves, we know others, too. "It is not the desert island nor the stony wilderness that cuts you off from the people you love," Anne Morrow Lindbergh[2] wrote in her book *Gift from the Sea*. "It is the wilderness in the mind, the desert wastes in the heart through which one wanders lost and a stranger."

The Sense of Joy. The further we go into ourselves the closer we come to one of meditation's greatest gifts: joy. "We don't meditate to withdraw," an instructor told me, "but to enjoy life." Indeed, our real selves, when they appear, often seem to be naturally joyous. Long ago, the philosopher Plotinus[3] wrote: "There is always a radiance[4] in the soul of man, untroubled, like the light in a lantern in a wild turmoil of wind and tempest."

---

1. correspondent: a person who writes to a magazine or newspaper, expressing an opinion, as on public affairs
2. Anne Morrow Lindbergh: 미국 최초의 여류 비행사로 남편과 함께 대서양을 횡단하고 5대륙 항로개척 비행을 하는 등 많은 업적을 남겼으며, 그에 따른 활발한 저술활동을 펼쳤다.
3. Plotinus: (205~270) 고대 철학자로 3세기 로마의 영향력 있는 지식인, 문필가 집단의 중심인물 이었다.
4. radiance: the quality or state of being radiant; brightness

The Infinite. The end product of meditation is increased awareness—of ourselves and of our fellow men, and also of the vibrating world around us. "Every day I took the ferryboat to work," a West Coast businessman told me, "but I hardly saw the ocean. If I look up from my paper, I felt that I saw nothing new or different. After I began meditating, though, I often sat on deck and really looked. And what a different ocean I saw—amber[1], silver, green, black, changing every minute!"

If we think long and lovingly about the world, we find ourselves plunging into it, sensing it, feeling it, and even the very stones and hills seem vividly alive. We find a meaning in everything—the seed in the ground, the bark on the tree, the sound of the ticket.

And even as meditation can bring us to an awareness of the living world, so with one more step it can take us to the borders of that invisible world which haunts[2] our lives like the perfume of unseen roses. We know, as psychologist Claudio Naranjo[3] writes, that we are "a part of the cosmos, a tide in the ocean of life, a chain in the network of processes that do not either begin or end within the enclosure of our skins. In one way or another[4], we spend our lives trying to find this web of kinship, which joins us to all living things and to God."

When meditation brings us to the verge of this world, it is brother to[5] prayer. It allows us to believe that the kingdom of heaven really is within us and that there is a linkage between our minds and whatever governs the world.

Meditation is not a cure-all. Properly used, however, it can give us back the wonderland of our minds: the happiness that children find in dreaming alone in an apple tree; the joy of sages for whom wisdom is the "pearl of great price." Through the centuries, it has taken thousands of people to the very edge

---

1. amber: a yellow or brownish-yellow translucent fossil resin found along some seacoasts and used in jewerly pipestems, etc. 호박색, 황갈색
2. haunt: to be associated with; fill atmosphere of; pervade (생각 따위가) ~에게 끊임없이 붙어 다니다, ~을 괴롭히다
3. Claudio Naranjo: 칠레 태생의 심리학자로 인간의 정신과 영혼을 연관지어 새로운 정신요법을 개발했다.
4. one way or another: 그래저래; 그럭저럭
5. be brother to: ~와 유사하다, 맞먹다

of a different land, returning them to life with renewed strength and purpose. Today there is a widespread feeling that the world of tomorrow should be very different from the world of today. Meditation is seen as a prelude to that transformation—a way of preparing for it, a way of changing lives and thus changing the world.

AFTER YOU READ

1. Where do many of today's meditators find their inspiration?

2. What do you define meditation?

3. What does Aldous Huxley write about meditation?

4. Where does experienced meditators meditate best?

5. How does meditation can help solve day-to-day problems?

6. What is meditation's great gift?

7. What is the ultimate result of meditation?

10

WHAT IS REALISM?

J. M. Coetzee[1]

Three is first of all the problem of the opening, namely how to get us from where we are, which is, as yet, nowhere, to the far bank. It is a simple bridging problem, a problem of knocking together[2] a bridge. People solve such problems every day. They solve them, and having solved them make a start.

So let us assume that, however it may be done, it is done. Let us take it that the bridge is built, that we have crossed it, we can leave it behind, forget it. We have left behind the territory in which we were. We are in the far territory, where we want to be.

Elizabeth Costello is a writer, born in 1927, which makes her sixty-nine years old, going on seventy. She had written nine novels, two books of poems, a book on the bird life of Queensland, and a body of journalism. By birth she is Australian. She was born in Melbourne and lives there today, but spent the years 1950 to 1962 abroad, in England and France. She has been married twice. She has two children, one by each marriage. Her son, John, who figures in this narratives, teaches in the Department of Astronomy at the Australian National University.

Elizabeth Costello made her name with her fourth novel, *The House on Eccles Street* (1969), whose main character is Marion Bloom, wife of Leopold Bloom, the principal character of

1. J. M. Coetzee: 2003년 노벨문학상을 수상한 쿳시는 1940년 남아프리카의 케이프타운에서 태어나 남아프리카와 미국에서 컴퓨터 과학자와 언어학자로 교육을 받았다. 그의 소설은 남아공의 인종차별을 다루고 있다.
2. If someone knocks two rooms or buildings into one or knocks them together, they make them form one room or building by removing a wall. 급히 만들다.

another novel, *Ulysses* (1922), by James Joyce. She has been widely honored, at home and abroad. There has even come into existence air Elizabeth Costello Society, based in Albuquerque, New Mexico, which puts out a quarterly *Elizabeth Costello Newsletter*.

In October of 1995 Elizabeth Costello travelled, or travels (present tense henceforth), to Waltham, Massachusetts, to Appleton college, to receive the Appleton Award. This award is made biennially to a major world writer, selected by a jury of eminent critics and writers. It consists of a purse[1] of $100,000, funded by a bequest from the Stowe estate, and a gold medal. It is one of the larger literary prizes in the United States.

On her visit to Massachusetts Elizabeth Costello (Costello is her maiden name) is accompanied by her son. She has become a little frail: without him she would not undertake this taxing trip across half the world and across two seasons.

We skip. They have reached Waltham and have been conveyed to their hotel, a surprisingly large building for a small city, a tall hexagon, all dark marble outside and crystal and mirrors inside. In her room a dialogue takes place.

"Will you be comfortable?" asks the son.

"I'm sure I will," she replies. Her room is on the twelfth floor, with a prospect over a golf course. Beyond are wooded hills.

"Then why not have a rest? They are fetching us at six-thirty. I'll give you a call a few minutes beforehand."

He is about to leave. She speaks.

"John, what do you want from me?"

"Tonight? Nothing. It's just a dinner with the jury. We won't let it turn into a long evening. I'll remind them you are tired."

"And tomorrow?"

"Tomorrow is a different story. You'll have to gird your loins[2] for tomorrow, I'm afraid."

"I've forgotten why I agreed to come. It seems a great ordeal to put oneself through, for no good reason. I should have told them to forget the ceremony and send the check in the mail."

After the long flight, she is looking her age. She has never taken care of her appearance; she used to be able to get away

1. purse: 기부금
2. gird your loins: 정신차리다

with it[1]; now it shows. Old and tired.

"It doesn't work that way, I'm afraid, Mother. If you want the money, you must go through with the show."

She shakes her head. She is still wearing the old blue raincoat she wore from the airport. Her hair has a greasy, lifeless look. She has made no move to unpack. If he leaves her now, what will she do? Lie down in her raincoat and shoes?

He is here, with her, out of love. He cannot imagine her getting through this trial without him at her side. He stands by her because he is her son, her loving son. But he is also on the point of becoming—distasteful word—her trainer.

He thinks of her as a seal, an old, tired circus seal. One more time she must heave herself up onto the tub, one more time show that she can balance the ball on her nose. Up to him to coax her, put heart in her, get her through the performance.

At six-thirty he knocks. She is ready, waiting, full of doubts but prepared to face the foe. She wears her blue costume and silk jacket, her lady novelist's uniform, and the white shoes with which there is nothing wrong yet which somehow make her look like Daisy Duck. She has washed her hair and brushed it back. It still looks greasy, but honorably greasy, like a navvy's or mechanic's[2]. Already on her face a passive look that, if you saw it in a young girl, you would call withdrawn. A face without personality, the kind that photographers have to work on to lend distinction. Like Keats, he thinks, the great advocate of blank receptiveness.

The blue costume, the greasy hair, these are details, signs of a moderate realism. Supply the particulars, allow the significations to emerge of themselves. A procedure pioneered by Daniel Defoe. Robinson Crusoe, cast up on the beach, looks around for his shipmates. But there are none. "I never saw them afterwards, or any sign of them," says he, "except three of their hats, one cap, and two shoes that were not fellows." Two shoes, not fellows: by not being fellows, the shoes have ceased to be footwear and become proofs of death, torn by the foaming seas off the feet of

---

1. get away with it: 멋지게 해내다, 무난히 해내다.

2. like a navvy's or mechanic: 운하공사의 인부나 기계공의 기름 낀 머리 같이; 일하다가 어쩔 수 없이 묻게 된; 명예로운의 뜻이 있음.

drowning men and tossed ashore. No large woods, no grief and despair, just hats and caps and shoes.

For as far back as she can remember, his mother has secluded herself in the mornings to do her writing. No intrusions under any circumstances. He used to think of herself as a misfortunate child, lonely and unloved. When they felt particularly sorry for themselves, he and his sister used to slump outside the locked door, making tiny whining sounds. In time the whining would change to brimming or singing, and they would feel better, forgetting their forsaken-ness.

Now the scene has changed. He has grown tip. He is no longer outside the door but inside, observing her as she sits, back to the window, confronting, day after day, year after year, while her hair slowly goes from black to gray, the blank page. What doggedness! She deserves the medal, he thinks, this one and many more. For valor beyond the call of duty.

The change came when she was thirty-three. Until then he had not read a word she had written. That was his reply to her, his revenge on her for locking him out. She denied him, therefore he denied her. Or perhaps he refused to read her in order to protect himself. Perhaps that was the deeper motive: to ward off[1] the lightning stroke. Then one day, without a word to anyone, without even a word to himself, he took one of her books out of the library. After that he read everything, reading openly, on the train, at the lunch table. "What are you reading?" "One of my mother's books"

He is in her books, or some of them. Other people, too, he recognizes; and there must be many more he does not recognize. About sex, about passion and jealousy and envy, she writes with an insight that shakes him. It is positively indecent.

She shakes him; that is what she presumably does to other readers too. That is presumably why, in the larger picture, she exists. What a strange reward for a lifetime of shaking people: to be conveyed to this town in Massachusetts and feted and given money! For she is by no means a comforting writer. She is even cruel, in a way that women can be but men seldom have the

1. To ward off a danger or illness means to prevent it from affecting you or harming you.

heart for. What sort of creature is she? Not a seal, certainly: not amiable enough for that. But not a shark either. A cat, perhaps. One of those large cats that pause as they eviscerate[1] their victim and, across the torn-open belly, give you a cold yellow stare.

There is scene in the restaurant, mainly dialogue, which I will skip. I pick up events back at the hotel, where Elizabeth Costello asks her son to run through the list again of the people they have just met. He obeys, giving each a name and function, as in life. Their host, William Brautegam, is dean of arts at Appleton. The convener of the jury, Gordon Wheatley, is a Canadian, a professor at McGill, who has written on Canadian literature and on Wilson Harris. The one they call Toni, who spoke to her about Henry Handel Richardson, is from Appleton College. She is a specialist on Australia and has taught there. Paula Sachs she knows. The bald man, Kerrigan, is a novelist, originally Irish, now living in New York. The fifth juror, the one who sat next him, is named Moebius. She teaches in California and edits a journal. She has also published stories.

"You and she had quite a tête-à-tête," says his mother. "Attractive, isn't she?"

"I suppose so."

She reflects. "But, as a group, don't they strike you as rather..."

"Rather lightweight?

She nods.

"Well, they are. The heavyweight aren't interested in this kind of show. The heavyweights are wrestling with heavy weight problems."

"I'm not heavyweight enough for them?"

"No, you're heavyweight all right. Your failing is that you're not a problem. What you write hasn't been shown to be a problem. Once you present a problem, you might be shifted over into their court. But for the present you're not a problem, just an example."

"An example of what?"

"An example of writing. An example of how someone of your station and your generation and your origins writes. An

1. To eviscerate a person or animal means to remove their internal organs, such as their heart, lungs, and stomach.

instance."

"An instance. Am I allowed to protest? After all the effort I put into not writing like anyone else?"

"Mother, there's no point in picking on[1] me to argue with. But you must surely concede that at a certain level we write like everyone else. Otherwise we would be writing private languages. It's not absurd—is it?—to be interested in what people have in common rather than in what sets them apart."

There is another literary debate the next morning. John goes down to the hotel gymnasium and there bumps into Gorden Wheatley, chairman of the jury. Side by side on exercise bicycles they have a shouted conversation. His mother will be disappointed, he tells Wheatley, not entirely seriously, if she hears she has won the Appleton Award because 1995 is the year of Australasia[2].

"What does she want hear?" shouts Wheatley back.

"That she is the best," he replies. "In you jury's honest opinion. No the best X or Y, just the best."

"Without infinity you can't do mathematics," shouts Whitley. "But that doesn't mean that infinity exists. It's just a construct[3], a human construct. Of course we say that Elizabeth Costello is the best. We just have to be clear what a statement like that means, in the context of our times."

The analogy with infinity makes no sense to him, but he does not pursue the argument. He hopes that Wheatley does not write as badly as he thinks.

Realism has never been comfortable with ideas. It could not be otherwise: realism is premised on the idea that ideas have no separate existence, can exist only in things. So when it needs to debate ideas, as here, it is driven to invent situations—walks in the countryside, conversations _ in which characters give voice to contending ideas and thereby in a certain sense embody them. The notion of embodying is cardinal. In these debates, ideas do not and indeed cannot float free: they are tied to the speakers by whom they are enounced, are generated from the matrix of individual interests out of which their speakers act in the world.

---

1. If someone picks on you, they repeatedly criticize you unfairly or treat you unkindly. 괴롭히다
2. Australasia: 오스트레일리아와 그 부근의 남양군도의 총칭
3. construct: 복합개념

Thus, for instance, the son's concern that his mother not be treated like a Mickey Mouse Third World writer, or Wheatley's concern not to seem an old-fashioned absolutist.

At eleven he taps on the door of his mother's room. They have a heavy schedule before them: an interview, a trip to the college radio station for a recording session, then, in the evening, the presentation ceremony and the speech that goes with it.

At the radio station the two of them are separated. He is shown into the control booth. The interviewer, he is surprised to see, is the elegant Moebius woman he had sat beside at dinner. "This is Susan Moebus, the program is *Writers at Work*, and we are speaking today to Elizabeth Costello," she says. She proceeds to give a crisp introduction. "Your most recent novel," she continues, "called *Fire and Ice*, is set in the Australia of the 1930s and is the story of a young man struggling to make his way as a painter, against the opposition of family and society. Did you have anyone in particular in mind when you wrote it? Does it draw upon[1] your own early life?"

"No, I was still a child in the 1930s. Of course we draw upon our own lives all the time—they are all we have. But no, *Fire and Ice* isn't autobiography. It's a work of fiction. I made it up."

"It's a powerful book, I must tell our listeners. But do you find it easy, writing from the position of a man?"

It is a routine question, opening the door to one of her routine paragraphs. To his surprise, she does not take the opening.

"Easy? No. If it were easy it wouldn't be worth doing. It's the otherness that is the challenge. Making up someone other than yourself. Making up a world for him to move in. Making up an Australia."

"Is that what you are doing in your books, would you say—making up Australia?"

"Yes, I suppose so. But it's not so easy nowadays. There's more resistance, a weight of other Australias made up by other people, that you have to push against. That's what we mean by tradition, the beginnings of a tradition."

"I'd like to get on to *The House on Eccles Street*, which is the

1. If you draw on or draw upon something such as your skill or experience, you make use of it in order to do something. ~을 참고로 하다

book you are best known for in this country, a pathbreaking book, and the figure of Molly Bloom. Critics have concentrated on the way you have claimed or reclaimed[1] Molly from Joyce, made her your own. I wonder if you would comment on your intentions in this book, particularly in challenging Joyce, one of the great father figures of modern literature, on his own territory."

Another clear opening, and this time she takes it.

"Yes, she is an engaging person, isn't she, Molly Bloom Joyce's Molly, I mean. She leaves her trace across the pages of *Ulysses* as a bitch in heat leaves her smell. Seductive you can't call it; it's cruder than that. Men pick up the scent and sniff and stare and circle around and snarl at each other, even when Molly isn't on the scene.

"No, I don't see myself as challenging Joyce. But with certain books there is such prodigal[2] inventiveness that there is material left over when the action is finished. Material that almost invites you to take it up and build something of your own."

"But you've taken Molly out of the house—if I can pick up on your metaphor taken her out of the house on Eccles Street where her husband and her lover and in a certain sense her author have confined her, where they turned her into a kind of queen bee, unable to fly, and turned her loose on the streets of Dublin. Wouldn't you see that as a challenge on your part, a response?"

"Queen bee, bitch . . . Let's revise the figure and call her a lioness, rather, stalking the streets, smelling the smells, seeing the sights. Looking for prey, even. Yes, I wanted to liberate her from that house, and particularly from that bedroom, with its creaking bedsprings, and turn her loose—as you say—on Dublin."

"If you see Molly Joyce's Molly—as a prisoner in *the house on Eccles Street*, do you see women in general as prisoners of marriage and domesticity?"

"You can't mean women today. But, yes, to an extent Molly is a prisoner of marriage, of the kind of marriage that was available in Ireland in 1904. Her husband, Leopold, is a prisoner too. If

1. If you reclaim something that you have lost or that has been taken away from you, you succeed in getting it back.
2. prodigal: 통이 큰, 풍부한

she is shut into the conjugal home, he is shut out. So we have Odysseus trying to get in and Penelope trying to get out. That's the comedy, the comic myth, which Joyce and I in our different ways paid our respects to."

Because both women are wearing earphones, addressing the microphone rather than each other, it is hard for him to see how they are getting on[1]. But he is impressed, as ever, by the persona his mother manages to project: of genial common sense, lack of malice, yet of sharp-witted-ness too.

"I wanted to tell you," the interviewer continues (a cool voice, he thinks: a cool woman, capable, not a lightweight at all), "what an impact *The House on Eccles Street* made on me when I first read it. I was a student, I had studied Joyce's book, I had absorbed the famous Molly Bloom episode and the critical orthodoxy that came with it, namely that here Joyce had released the authentic voice of the feminine, the sensual reality of woman, and so forth. And then I read your book and realized that Molly didn't have to be limited in the way Joyce had shown her, that she could equally well be an intelligent woman with an interest in music and a circle of friends of her own and a daughter with whom she shared confidences—it was a revelation, as I say. And I began to wonder about other women whom we think of as having been given a voice by male writers in the name of their liberation, yet in the end only to speak and serve a male philosophy. I am thinking of D. H. Lawrence's women in particular, but if you go further back they might include Tess of the D'Urbervilles and Anna Karenina, to name just two. It's a huge question, but I wonder if you have anything to say about it—not just about the lives of Marion Bloom but about the project of reclaiming women's lives in general."

"No, I didn't think there's anything I would want to say, I think you've said it all very fully. Of course, fair's fair, men will have to set about reclaiming the Heathcliffs and Rochesters from romantic stereotyping too, to say nothing of poor old dusty Casaubon. It will be grand spectacle. But seriously, we can't go on parasitizing the classics forever. I'm not excluding myself from the charge. We've got to do some inventing of our own."

1. getting on: proceeding

We skip to the evening, to the main event, the presentation of the award. Elizabeth Costello's son John finds himself in the first row of the audience, among the special guests. The woman to his left introduces herself. "Out daughter is at Appleton," she says. "She is writing her honors dissertation on your mother. She's a great fan. She has made us read everything." She pats the wrist of the man beside her: her husband. They have the look of money, old money. Benefactors, no doubt. "Your mother is much admired in this country," she says. "Particularly by young people. You should tell her that."

All across America, young women writing dissertation on his mother. Adherents, disciples. Would it really please her to be told? The presentation scene itself I will skip. Generally speaking, it is not a good idea to interrupt the narratives too often, since storytelling works by lulling the reader or listener into a dream state in which real-world time and space fade away, superseded by the time and space of the fiction. Breaking into the dream draws attention to the constructedness of the story and plays havoc with[1] the realist illusion. However, unless I skip certain scenes we will be here all day. The skips are not part of the text, they are part of the performance.

The award is made. Then his mother is left alone at the rostrum to give her acceptance speech, which in the program is entitled, "at Is realism?" The time has arrived for her to perform, to show her mettle[2].

She puts on her glasses. "Ladies and gentlemen," she says, and begins to read.

"I published my first book in 1955, forty years ago. I was living in London, at that time the cultural metropolis for Australians. I remember clearly the day when a package arrived in the mail, a copy of the book, an advance copy. I was of course thrilled to have it in my hands at last, the real thing. But there was still one thing that nagged me. I got on the telephone to my publishers. 'Have the deposit copies gone out? I asked. And I would not rest until I had their assurance that the deposit copies would be

1. play havoc with: 못쓰게 만들다
2. Someone's mettle is their ability to do something well in difficult circumstances. 열정, 기질

mailed the same afternoon, to the Bodleian and the other places, but above all to the British Museum. That was my great ambition: to have a place on the shelves of the British Museum, rubbing shoulders with the great C's: Carlyle and Chaucer and Coleridge and Conrad. (The joke is that my closest literary neighbor turned out to be Marie Corelli.)

"One smiles now at such ingenuousness. Yet behind my anxiety there was something serious, and behind that seriousness in turn something pathetic that is less easy to acknowledge.

"Let me explain. Besides all the copies of the book you have written that are going to perish—that are going to be pulped because there is no sale for them, that are going to be opened and read for a page or two and then yawned at and put aside forever, that are going to be left behind at seaside hotels or in trains—besides all these lost ones we must be able to feel there is at least one copy that will not only be read but be taken care of, given a home, given a place on the shelf that will be its own in perpetuity. What lay behind my anxiety about deposit copies was the wish that, even if I should be knocked over by a bus the next day, this firstborn of mine would have a home where it could snooze[1] for the next hundred years, and no one would come poking with a stick to see if it was still alive.

"That was one side of my telephone call: if I, this mortal shell, was going to die, let me at least live on through my creations." Elizabeth Costello proceeds to reflect on the transience of fame, the transience even of deposit libraries. I skip, and resume. "Let me now turn to my subject, 'What Is Realism?'

"There is a story by Franz Kafka[2] in which an ape, dressed up for the occasion, makes a speech to a learned society. It is a speech, but a test too, an examination, a viva voce. He has to show not only that he can speak his audience's language but that he has mastered their manners and conventions, is fit to enter their society. Why am I reminding you of Kafka's story? Am

---

1. snooze: doze
2. Franz Kafka: 1883년 프라하의 유태인 가정에서 출생했다. 1917년에 폐결핵 진단을 받았으며, 이후 <성>등을 쓰다가 건강이 악화되어 결핵 요양소에서 1924년 사망했다. 오늘날 실존주의의 주요작가로 평가받으며, 인간의 불안과 부조리를 문학으로 형상화하여 높은 지지를 받는다. <변신>이 가장 유명하며, <심판> <유형지에서>등도 대표작이다.

I going to pretend I am the ape, torn away from my natural surroundings, forced to perform in front of gathering of critical strangers? I hope not. I am one of you, I am not of different species. "Those of you who know the story will remember that it is cast in the form of a monologue, a monologue by the ape. There is thus no means, within the world of the story, for either speaker or audience to be scrutinized with an outsider's eye. For all we know, the speaker may not 'really' be an ape, may be simply a human being like ourselves deluded into thinking himself an ape, or a human being presenting himself, with heavy irony, for rhetorical purposes, as an ape. For all we know, too, the audience may consists not, as we imagine, of bewhiskered, red-faced gents who have put aside their bush jackets and topis for evening dress, but of fellow apes, trained, if not to the level of our speaker, who can mouth complicated sentences in German, then at least to sit and listen; or, if not trained to that pitch, then chained to their seats and trained not to jabber[1] and pick fleas and relieve themselves openly.

"We don't know. We don't know and will never know, with certainty, what is really going on in this story: whether it is a man speaking to men or an ape speaking to apes or an ape speaking to men or a man speaking to apes (though the last is, I think, unlikely) or even just a parrot speaking to parrots.

"There used to be a time when we knew. We used to believe that when the text said, 'On the table stood a glass of water,' there was indeed a glass of water, and a table, and we had only look in the word-mirror of the text to see them both.

"But all that has ended. The word-mirror is broken, irreparably, it seems. About what is really going on in the lecture hall your guess is as good as mine: men and men, men and apes, apes and men, apes and apes, whatever. The lecture hall itself may be nothing but a zoo. The words on the page will no longer stand up and be counted, each saying, 'I mean what I mean!' The dictionary that used to stand beside the Bible and the works of Shakespeare above the fireplace, in the place occupied by the household gods in pious Roman homes, has become just one code

1. If you say that someone is jabbering, you mean that they are talking very quickly and excitedly, and you cannot understand them.

book among many.

"This is the situation in which I appear before you. I am not using the privilege of this platform to make idle, nihilistic jokes about what I am, ape or woman, and what you are, my auditors. That is not the point of the story, say I, who am nevertheless in no position to dictate[1] what the point of story is. There used be a time, we believe, when we could say who we were. Now we are just performers, speaking our parts. The bottom has dropped out. We could think of this as a tragic turn of events, were it not that it is hard to have respect for whatever the bottom was that dropped out—it looks to us like an illusion now, one of those illusions sustained only by the concentrated gaze of everyone in the room. As soon as you look away, the mirror falls to the floor and shatters.

"There is every reason, then, for me to feel less than certain about myself as I stand before you. Despite this splendid award, for which I am deeply grateful, despite the promise it make that, gathered into the illustrious company of those who have won it before me, I am beyond the reach of time's envious grasp, we all know, if we are being realistic, that is only a matter of time before the books which you honor, and with whose genesis I have had something to do, will ceased to be read and eventually ceased to be remembered. And properly so. There is a limit to the burden of remembering we can impose on our children and grandchildren. They will have a world of their own, of which we will be less and less part. Thank you."

The applause starts hesitantly, but then swells. His mother takes off her glasses, smiles. It is an engaging smile: she seems to be relishing the moment. Actors bathe in applause like this all the time, ill deserved or well deserved: actors, singers, violinists. Why should she not have her moment of glory too?

The applause dies down. Dean Brautegam leans into the microphone. "There will be refreshments[2]—"

"Excuse me!" A clear, confidant young voice cuts through the dean's.

There is a flurry in the audience. Heads are turning. "There

1. dictate: 지시하다
2. refreshments: 다과, 청량음료

will be refreshments in the foyer, and a exhibition of Elizabeth Costello's books. Please join us there. It remains for me -"

"Excuse me!"

"Yes!"

"I have a question."

The speaker is standing up: a young woman in a white T-shirt. Brautegam is cleary nonplused[1]. As for his mother, she has lost her smile. He knows her look. She has had enough now, she wants to be away.

"I am not sure," says Brautegam, frowning, looking around for support. "Our format tonight does not allow for questions. I would like to thank -"

"Excuse me! I have a question for the speaker. May I address the speaker?"

There is a hush. All eyes are on Elizabeth Costello. Frostily she gazes into the distance.

Brautegam pulls himself together.[2] "I would like to thank Ms. Costello, whom we have gathered tonight to honor. Please join us in the foyer. Thank you." And he switches off the microphone.

There is a buzz of talk as they leave the auditorium. An incident, no less. He can see the girl in the white T-shirt ahead of him in the throng. She walks stiff and erect and seemingly angry. What was the question going to be? Would it not have been better to have it aired?

He fears that the scene will repeat itself in the foyer. But there is no scene. The girl has left, gone out into the night, perhaps stormed out. Nevertheless, the incident leaves a bad taste; say what one might, the evening has been spoiled.

What was she going to ask? People huddle together, whispering. They seemed to have a shrewd idea. He has a shrewd idea too. Something to do with what Elizabeth Costello the famous writer might have been expected to say on an occasion like this, and did not say.

He can see Dean Brautegam and others fussing around his mother now, trying to smooth things over. After all they have

---

1. If you are nonplussed, you feel confused and unsure how to react.(= at a loss)
2. If you are upset or depressed and someone tells you to pull yourself together they are telling you to control your feelings and behave calmly again.

invested, they want her to go home thinking well of them and of Appleton College. Nevertheless, they must already be glancing ahead to 1997, hoping that the 1977 jury will come up with a more winning winner.

I skip the rest of the foyer scene, move back to the hotel.

Elizabeth Costello retires for the night. Her son, who is in many ways the main actor henceforth, watches television in his room, then grows restless and goes down to the lounge. There, for the second time that day, he sees the woman who interviewed his mother for radio, Susan Moebius. She waves him over. She is with a companion, but the companion soon departs, leaving the two of them alone.

He finds her attractive. She dresses well, better than the conventions of the academy permit. She has long, golden blond hair; she sits upright in her chair, squaring her shoulders; when she tosses her hair, the movement is quite queenly.

They skirt[1] the events of the evening. They speak about the revival of radio as a cultural medium. "An interesting session you had with my mother," he says. "I know you've written a book about her, which I haven't read—I'm sorry. Do you have good things to say about her?"

"I hope I do. She is a key writer for our times. The book isn't about her alone, but she figures strongly in it."

"But is she a key writer for all of us, or just for women? I got the feeling during the interview that you see her as a woman writer or a woman's writer. Would you still consider her a key writer if she were a man?"

"If she were a man?"

"All right: if you were a man?"

"If I were a man? I don't know. I've never been a man. I'll let you know when I've tried it."

They smile. There is definitely something in the air.

"But my mother has been a man," he persists. "She has also been a dog. She can think her way into other people, into other existences. I've read her; I know. It's within her powers. Isn't that what's most important about fiction, that it takes us out of ourselves, into other lives?"

1. If you skirt a problem or question, you avoid dealing with it.

"Perhaps. But your mother remains a woman all the time. Whatever she does, she does as a woman. She inhibits her characters as a woman does, not a man."

"I don't see that. I find her men perfectly believable."

"You don't see because you wouldn't see. Only a woman would see. It's something between women. If her men are believable, good, I'm glad to hear so, but finally it's just mimicry. Women are good at mimicry, better than men. At parody, even. We have a lighter touch."

She is smiling again. See how light my touch can be, her lips seem to say. Soft lips.

"If there's parody in her," he says, "it's too subtle for me to pick up." There is a long silence. "So is that what you think," he says at last, "that we live parallel lives, men and women, that we never really meet?"

The drift of the conversation has changed. They are no longer speaking about writing, if they ever were.

"What do you think?" she says. "What does your experience tell you? And is difference such a bad thing? If there were no differences, what would happen to desire?"

They are alone in the elevator. Not the elevator he is used to: a different shaft[1]. Which is north, which south, in this hexagon of a hotel, this beehive. He presses the woman against the wall, kisses her, tasting smoke on her breath. Research: will that be her name for it afterward? Using a secondary source? He kisses her again, she kisses him back, kissing flesh of the flesh.

They exit on the thirteenth floor. He follows her down a corridor, turning right and left.. He loses track. Where is it, the core of the hive? His mother's room is 1254. His is 1220. Hers is 1307. He did not know there was a thirteenth floor. He thought that floors went from twelve to fourteen, that that was the rule in the hotel world. Where is 1307 in relation to 1254: north, south, west, east?

I skip again, a skip this time in the text rather than in the performance.

When he thinks back over those hours, one moment comes back with sudden force, the moment when her knee slips under

1. A shaft is a long vertical passage, for example for a lift.

his arm and folds into[1] his armpit. A shapely thigh, he thinks, appraising, approving. Curious that the night should be dominated by a single recollection, not obviously significant, yet so strong that he can almost feel the ghostly knee against his skin. Does the mind by nature prefer sensations to ideas, the tangible to the abstract? Or is her knee just a mnemonic, from which will unfold the rest of the night?

They are lying in the dark, flank to flank[2], in the text of memory, talking.

"So, has it been a successful visit?" she asks.

"From whose point of view?"

"Yours."

"My point of view doesn't matter. I came for Elizabeth Costello's sake. Hers is the point of view that matters. Yes, successful. Successful enough."

"Do I detect a touch of bitterness?"

"None. I'm here to help—that's all."

"It's very good of you. Do you feel you owe her something?"

"Yes. filial duty. It' s perfectly natural among humankind."

She ruffles his hair. "Don't be cross," she says.

"I'm not."

She slides down beside him, strokes him. "Successful enough—what does that mean?" she murmurs. She is not giving up. A price has yet to be paid for this time in her bed, for this conquest.

"The speech didn't come off. She was disappointed. She put a lot of work into it."

"There was nothing wrong with the speech in itself. But the tide was mystifying. And she shouldn't have used Kafka. There are better texts."

"Are there?"

"Yes, better, more suitable. This is America, the 1990s. People don't want to hear the Kafka thing yet again."

"What do you want to hear then?"

She shrugs. "Something more personal. Not necessarily more intimate. But audiences don't react well to heavy historical self-ironization anymore. They might at a pinch accept it from a man,

1. folds into his armpit;감싸다, 껴안다
2. flank to flank; 옆에 나란히

but not from a woman. A woman doesn't need all that armor."

"And a man does?"

"You tell me. If it's a problem, it's a male problem. We didn't give the award to a man."

"Have you considered the possibility that my mother has got beyond the male-female opposition? That she has explored it as far as it will go, and is now after larger game?"

"Such as?"

The hand that has been stroking him has paused. The moment is important, he knows. She is waiting for his answer, for the privileged access it promises. He can feel the thrill of the moment, electric, reckless.

"Such as measuring herself against the illustrious dead. Such as paying tribute to the powers that animate her. For instance."

"Is that what she says?"

"You don't think that is what she has been doing throughout her life—measuring herself against the masters? Has no one in the profession recognize that?"

He should not be saying this. He should be keeping out of his mother's business. He is in a stranger's bed not for his bonny[1] blue eyes but because he is his mother's son. Yet here he is spilling the beans like a nincompoop! He sees now how spy-women work. Nothing subtle to it. The man is seduced not because his will to resist is overcome but because being seduced is a pleasure in itself. He falls in order to fall, for the pleasure of falling.

He wakes once during the night, in a state of deep sadness, such sadness he wants to cry. He touches the naked shoulder of the woman beside him, but she does not respond. Lightly he runs a hand down her body, breast, flank, hip, thigh, knee. Handsome in every detail, in a blank kind of way.

He has a vision of his mother in her big double bed, crouched in sleep, her knees drawn tip, her back bared. Out of her back, out of the waxy, old person's flesh, protrude three needles: not the tiny needles of the acupuncturist or the voodoo doctor, but thick, gray needles, steel or plastic: knitting needles. the needles have not killed her, there is no need to worry about that, she breathes

1. Someone or something that is bonny is attractive and nice to look at. (=lovely)

regularly. Nevertheless, she lies impaled.

Who has done it? Who would have done it?

Such loneliness, he thinks, hovering over the old woman in the bare room. His heart is breaking; the sadness pours down like a gray waterfall behind his eyes.

He should never have come here, to room thirteen whatever it is. A wrong move. He ought get up at once, steal out. But he does not. Why? Because he does not want to be alone. And because he wants to sleep. Sleep, he thinks, that knits up the ravelled sleeve of care. What an extraordinary way of phrasing[1] it! Not all the monkeys in the world, picking away at typewriters all their lives, would come up with those words. Out of the dark emerging, out of nowhere: first not there, then there, like a new born child, heart working, brain working, all the processes of that intricate electrochemical labyrinth working. A miracle. He closes his eyes.

She is already at breakfast when he comes down. She is wearing white, she looks rested and content. He joins her. From her purses she takes something and lays it on the table.: his watch. "It's eight hours off," she says. "Not eight," he says. "Sixteen. Canberra time. So that I won't forget who I really am."

Her eyes rest on his, or his on hers. Green-flecked. He feels a tug. A continent still unexplored, and he about to leave! A pang, a tiny pang of loss, shoots through him. Pain not without pleasure, like certain grades of toothache. He can conceive of something quite serious with this woman, whom he will not see again.

"I know what you are thinking," she says. "You are thinking we won't see each other again. You are thinking, What a wasted investment."

"What else do you see?"

"You think I have been using you. You think I have been trying to reach your mother through you."

She is smiling. No fool. A capable player.

"Yes, he says. "No." He draws a deep breath. I'll tell you what I really think. I think you are drawn, even if you won't acknowledge it, by the mystery of the divine in the human. You know there is something special in my mother, yet when you

---

1. If you phrase something in a particular way, you express it in words in that way. 표현하다

meet her, she turns out to be just an ordinary old woman. You can't square the two. You want an explanation. You want a clue, a sign, if not from her, then from me. That's what you think. It' all right, I don't mind." Strange words to be speaking over breakfast, over coffee and toast. He did not know he had them in him.

"You really are her son, aren't you. Do you write too?"

"You mean, am I touched by the god? No. But yes, I am her son. Not a foundling, not an adoptee. Out of her very body I came, caterwauling[1]."

"Will I have a chance to say goodby to your mother?" "You can catch her before the television interview. It's at ten, in the ballroom."

The television people have chosen the ballroom because of the red velvet drapes. In front of the drapes they have set up a rather ornate chair for her, and a smaller chair for the woman who will ask the questions. Susan, when she comes, has to cross the whole length of the room. She is ready to travel; she has a calf-leather satchel over her shoulder; her stride is easy, confidant. Again the pang comes, but light as a feather.

"It's been a great honor to get to know you, Mrs. Costello," she says, taking his mother's hand.

"Elizabeth," says his mother. "Excuse the throne."

"Elizabeth."

"I want to give you this," says Susan Moebius, and from her satchel produces a book. The cover show a woman wearing an antique Grecian costume, holding a scroll. Reclaiming a History Women and Memory, says the title. Susan Kaye Moebius.

"Thank you, I look forward to reading it," says his mother.

At the end of the interview Susan Moebius's book is almost left behind. He is the one who picks it up from under her chair.

"I wish people wouldn't give one books," she murmurs. "Where am I going to find space for it?"

"I have space."

"Then you take it. Keep it. You're the one she is really after, not me."

---

1. If a person or animal caterwauls, they make a loud, high, unpleasant noise like the noise that cats make when they fight.

He reads the inscription: To Elizabeth Costello, with gratitude and admiration. "Me?" he says. "I don't think so. I am just"—his voice barely falters—"a pawn in the game. You are the one she loves and hates."

He barely falters; but the word that came to mind was not "pawn," it was "clipping." a toenail clipping[1], that one steals and winds up in a tissue and takes away.

His mother does not reply. But she does give him a smile, a quick, sudden smile of joy and—he cannot see it in any other way—triumph.

Their duties are over. The television crew are packing up. In half an hour a taxi will take them to the airport. She has won, more or less. On foreign turf too. An away win. She can go home bearing her true self, leaving behind an image, false, like all images.

What is the truth of his mother? He does not know, does not want to know. He is here simply to protect her, to bar the way against the relic seekers and the sentimental pilgrims. Yet there is also an impulse in him to speak out before he goes, to whoever will hear. This woman, he wants to say, whose words you hang on[2] as if she were the sibyl, is the same woman who, forty years ago, would lie in bed in her bed-sitter[3] in Hampstead all day, crying soundlessly to herself, crawling out in the evenings into the foggy streets to buy the fish and chips on which she lived, then falling asleep in her clothes. She is the same woman who stormed around the house in Melbourne, hair flying in all directions, screaming at her children, "You are killing me! You are tearing the flesh from my body!" (He lay in the dark with his sister afterward, comforting her while she sobbed: he was seven; it was his first experience of fatherhood) This is the secret world of the oracle. How can you understand her before you know who she really is; and how, knowing who she is, can you understand her?

He does not hate his mother. (As he thinks these words, other

---

1. A clipping is an article, picture, or advertisement that has been cut from a newspaper or magazine.
2. If one thing hangs on another, it depends on it in order to be successful. (=depend)
3. A bed-sitter is a room you rent which you use for both living in and sleeping in. (=bedsit)

words echo at the back of his mind; the words of one of William Faulkner's people insisting with mad receptiveness that he does not hate the South. Who is it?) He does not hate her. Quite the contrary. If he had hated her, he would long ago have put the greatest possible distance between the two of them. He does not hate her. He serves at her shrine, cleaning up after the excitement of the holy day, sweeping up the petals, collecting the offerings, putting the widows' mites[1] together, ready to bank. He may not share in the frenzy, but he worships too.

A mouthpiece for the divine. But "oracle" is not the right word. Not in the Greek mold. More like Tibet or India: a god reincarnated in a child, who is then wheeled from village to village, applauded, venerated.

Then they are in the taxi, driving through streets that already have the air of streets about to be forgotten.

"So," says his mother. "A clean getaway."

"I do believe so. Have you got the check?"

"The check, the medal, everything."

A gap. They are in Boston, at the airport, at the gate, waiting for the flight to be called that will take them on the next stage of their journey home. Faintly, over their heads, with a crude, driving hunt, a version of *Eine Kleine nachtmusik* is playing. Opposing them sits a woman eating popcorn out of a paper bucket, so fat that her feet barely touch the floor.

"Can I ask you one thing? he says. "Why realism? No one here wanted hear about it. Why such a grim subject?"

Fiddling in her purse, she says nothing.

"When I think of realism," he goes on, "I think of peasants frozen in blocks of ice. I think of Norwegians in smelly underwear. Why are you interested in that kind of thing? And where does Kafka fit in? What has Kafka to do with it?"

"With what? With smelly underwear.

"Yes. With smelly underwear. With people picking their noses. You don't write about it. Kafka didn't write about it."

"No, Kafka didn't write about picking their noses. But Kafka had time to wonder where and how his poor educated ape was going to find a mate. And what it was going to be like for him in

1. the widow's mite: 과부의 작은 연보금

the dark with the bewildered, half-tamed female that his keepers eventually produced for his use. Kafka's ape is embedded in life. It is the embeddedness that is important, not the life. His ape is embedded as we are embedded, you in me, I in you. The ape is followed through to the end, to the bitter, unsayable end, whether or not traces are left on the page. Kafka stays awake during the gaps when we are sleeping. That is where he fits in."

The fat woman is observing them frankly, her little eyes flickering from the one to the other: the old woman in the raincoat and the balding man who could be her son, having a fight in their funny accents.

"Well," he says, "if what you say is true, it's repulsive. It's zookeeping, not writing."

"What would you prefer? A zoo without keepers, where the animals fall into a trance when you stop looking at them? A zoo of ideas? A gorilla cage with the idea of a gorilla in it, an elephant cage with the idea of elephants in it? Do you know how many kilograms of solid waste an elephant drops in twenty-four hours? If you want a real elephant cage with real elephants, then you need a zookeeper to clean up after them."

"You're off the point, Mother. And don't get excited." He turns to the fat woman. "We're discussing literature, the claims of realism versus the claims of idealism."

Without ceasing to chew, the fat woman removes her eyes from them. He thinks of the cud[1] of mashed corn and saliva in her mouth, and shudders. Where doe it all end?

"There's a difference between cleaning up after animals and watching them while they do their business," he starts again. "We're talking about the latter, not the former. Don't animals deserve a private life as much as we do?"

"Not if they're in a zoo," she says. "Not if they're on show. Once you're on show, you have no private life. Anyway, do you ask permission from the stars before you peer at them through your telescope? What about the private lives of stars?"

"Mother, the stars are lumps of rock."

"Are they? I thought they were traces of light millions of years old."

---

1. cud: 씹는 음식의 한 입

"Boarding will now commence for flight 323, nonstop to Los Angeles," says a voice above their heads. "Passengers requiring assistance, as well as families with young children, may step forward."

On the flight she barely touches her food. She orders two brandies, one after the other, then falls asleep. When hours later, they begin the descent to Los Angeles, she is still asleep. The stewardess taps her on the shoulder. "Ma'am, your seat belt." She does not stir. They exchange looks, he and the stewardess. He leans across and clips the belt across her lap.

She lies slumped deep in her seat. Her head is sideways, her mouth open. She is snoring faintly. Light flashes from the windows as they bank[1], the sun setting brilliantly over southern California. He can see up her nostrils, into her mouth, down the back of her throat. And what he cannot see he can imagine: the gullet, pink and ugly, contracting as it swallows, like a python, drawing things down to the pear-shaped belly sac. He draws away, fastens his own belt, sits up, facing forward. No, he tells himself, that is not where I come from, that is not it.

1. When an aircraft banks, one of its wings rises higher than the other, usually when it is changing direction.

AFTER YOU READ

1. In October of 1995 Elizabeth Costello travelled to Waltham, Massachusetts. For what?

2. On her visit to Massachusetts, Elizabeth is accompanied by her son. Why?

3. Her son used to think of himself as a misfortunate child. Why?

4. After the award ceremony, Elizabeth made a speech on Realism. During the speech, she quote a certain writer's story. Whose story is it?

11

BEYOND THE MELTING POT

William A. Henry III

Some day soon surely much sooner than most people . . . realize, white Americans will become a minority group. Long before that day arrives, the presumption that the "typical" U.S. citizen is someone who traces his or her descent[1] in a direct line to Europe will be part of the past. By the time [today's] elementary [school] students . . . reach midlife, their diverse ethnic experience in the classroom will be echoed in neighborhoods and workplaces throughout the U.S.

Already 1 American in 4 defines himself or herself as Hispanic or nonwhite. If current trends in immigration and birth rates persist, the Hispanic population will have further increased an estimated 21%, the Asian presence about 22%, blacks almost 12%, and whites a little more than 2% when the 20th century ends. By 2020, a date no further into the future than John F. Kennedy's election is in the past, the number of U.S. residents who are Hispanic or nonwhite will have more than doubled, to nearly 115 million, while the white population will not be increasing at all. By 2056, when someone born today will be 66 years old, the "average" U.S. resident, as defined by Census statistics, will trace his or her decent to Africa, Asia, the Hispanic world, the Pacific Islands, Arabia—almost anywhere but white Europe.

While there may remain towns or outposts where even a black family will be something of an oddity, where English and

1. You use descent to talk about a person's family background for example their nationality or social status. (= origin, ancestry)

Irish and German surnames will predominate, where a traditional (some will wistfully say "real") America will still be seen on almost every street corner, they will be only the vestiges of an earlier nation. The former majority will learn, as a normal part of everyday life, the meaning of the Latin slogan engraved on U.S. coins — EPLURIBUS UNUM, one formed form many.

Among the younger populations that go to school and provide new entrants to the work force, the change will happen sooner. In some places an America beyond the melting pot has already arrived. In New York State some 40% of elementary and secondary-school children belong to an ethnic minority. Within a decade, the proportion is expected to approach 50%. In California white pupils are already a minority. Hispanics (who, regardless of their complexion, generally distinguish themselves from both blacks and whites) account for[1] 31.4% of public school enrollment, blacks add 8.9%, and Asians and others amount to 11%—for a nonwhite total of 51.3%. This finding is not only a reflection of white flight from desegregated public schools. Whites of all ages account for just 58% of California's population. In San Jose bearers of the Vietnamese surname Nguyen outnumber the Joneses in the telephone directory 14 columns to eight.

Nor is the change confined to the coasts. Some 12,000 Hmong refugees form Laos have settled in St. Paul. At some Atlanta low-rent apartment complexes that used to be virtually all black, social workers today need to speak Spanish. At the Sesame Hut restaurant in Houston, a Korean immigrant owner trains Hispanic immigrant workers to prepare Chinese-style food for a largely black clientele. The Detroit area has 200,000 people of Middle Eastern descent; some 1,500 small grocery and convenience stores in the vicinity are owned by a whole subculture of Chaldean Christians with roots in Iraq. "Once America was a microcosm of European nationalities," says Molefi Asante, chairman of the department of African-American studies at Temple University in Philadelphia. "Today America is a microcosm of the world."

History suggests that sustaining a truly multiracial society is difficult, or at least unusual. Only a handful of great powers of

---

1. If a particular thing account for a part or proportion of something, that part or proportion consists of that thing, or is used or produced by it.

the distant past — Pharaonic Egypt and Imperial Rome, most notably — managed to maintain a distant national identity while embracing, and being ruled by, an ethnic mélange. The most ethnically diverse contemporary power, the Soviet Union, is beset with secessionist demands and near tribal conflicts. But such comparisons are flawed, because those empires were launched by conquest and maintained through an aggressive military presence. The U.S. was created, and continues to be redefined, primarily by voluntary immigration. This process has been one of the country's great strengths, infusing it with talent and energy. The "browsing of America" offers tremendous opportunity for capitalizing[1] anew on the merits of many peoples from many lands. Yet this fundamental change in the ethnic makeup of the U.S. also poses risks. The American character is, resilient and thrives on change. But past periods of rapid evolution have also, alas, brought out deeper, more fearful aspects of national soul.

POLITICS: NEW AND SHIFTING ALLIANCES

A truly multiracial society will undoubtedly prove much harder to govern. Even seemingly race-free conflicts will be increasingly complicated by an overlay of ethnic tension. For example, the expected showdown in the early 21st century between the rising number of retirees and the dwindling number of workers who must be taxed to pay for the elders' Social Security benefits will probably be compounded by the fact that a large majority of recipients will be white, whereas a majority of workers paying for them will be nonwhite.

While prior generations of immigrants believed they had to learn English quickly to survive, many Hispanics now maintain that the Spanish language is inseparable from their ethnic and cultural identity, and seek to remain bilingual, if not primarily Spanish-speaking, for life. They see legislative drives to make English the sole official language, which have prevailed in some fashion in at least 16 states, as a political backlash. Says Arturo

1. If you capitalize on a situation, you use it to gain some advantage for yourself.

Vargas of the Mexican American Legal Defense and Educational Fund: "That's what English-only has been all about—a reaction to the growing population and influence of Hispanics. It's human nature to be uncomfortable with change. That's what the Census is all about, documenting changes and making sure the country keeps up."

Racial and ethnic conflict remains an ugly fact of American life everywhere, from working-class ghettos to college campuses, and those who do not raise their fists often raise their voices over affirmative action and other power sharing. When Florida Atlantic University, a state-funded institution under pressure to increase its low black enrollment, offered last month to give free tuition to every qualified black freshman who enrolled, the school was flooded with calls of complaint, some protesting that nothing was being done for "real" Americans. As the numbers of minorities increase, their demands for a share of the national bounty are bound to intensify, while whites are certain to feel ever more embattled. Businesses often feel whipsawed between immigration laws that punish them for hiring illegal aliens and anti-discrimination laws that penalize them for demanding excessive documentation from foreign-seeming job applicants. Even companies that consistently seek to do the right thing may be overwhelmed by the problems of diversifying a primarily white managerial corps fast enough to direct a work force that will be increasingly nonwhite and potentially, resentful.

Nor will tensions be limited to the polar simplicity of white vs. nonwhite. For all Jesse Jackson's rallying cries about shared goals, minority groups often feel keenly competitive. Chicago's Hispanic leaders have leapfrogged between white and black factions, offering support wherever there seemed to be the most to gain for their own community. Says Dan Solis of the Hispanic-oriented United Neighborhood Organization: "If you're thinking power, you don't put your eggs in one basket."

Blacks, who feel they waited longest and endured most in the fight for equal opportunity, are uneasy about being supplanted by Hispanics or, in some areas, by Asians as the numerically largest and most influential minority — and even more, about being outstripped in wealth and status by these newer groups. Because Hispanics are so numerous and Asians such a fast-growing group, they have become the "hot" minorities, and blacks feel their needs are getting lower priority. As affirmative action has broadened to include other groups — and to benefit white women perhaps most of all — blacks perceive it as having waned in value for them.

THE CLASSROOM: WHOSE HISTORY COUNTS?

Political pressure has already brought about sweeping change in public school textbooks over the past couple of decades and has begun to affect the core humanities curriculum at such élite universities as Standford. At stake at the college level is whether the traditional "canon" of Greek, Latin and West European humanities study should be expanded to reflect the cultures of Africa, Asia and other parts of the world. Many books treasured as classics by prior generations are now seen as tools of cultural imperialism. In the extreme form, this thinking rises to a value-deprived neutralism that views all cultures, regardless of the grandeur or paucity of their attainments, as essentially equal.

Even more troubling is a revisionist approach to history in which groups that have gained power in the present turn to remaking the past in the image of their desires. If 18th, 19th and earlier 20th century society should not have been so dominated by white Christian men of West European ancestry, they reason, then that past society should be reinvented as pluralist and democratic. Alternatively, the racism and sexism of the past are treated as inextricable from — and therefore irremediably tainting — traditional learning and values.

While debates over college curriculum get the most attention, professors generally can resist or subvert the most wrong-headed changes and students generally have mature enough judgment to sort out the arguments. Elementary- and secondary-school curriculums reach a far broader segment at a far more impressionable age, and political expediency[1] more often wins over

1. Expediency means doing what is convenient rather than what is morally right. (=convenience)

intellectual honesty. Exchanges have been vituperative[1] in New York, where a state task force concluded that "African-Americans, Asian-Americans, Puerto Ricans and Native Americans have all been victims of an intellectual and educational oppression. . . . Negative characterizations, or the absence of positive references, have had a terribly damaging effect on the psyche of young people." In urging a revised syllabus, the task force argued, "Children from European culture will have less arrogant perspective of being part of a group that has 'done it all.'" Many intellectuals are outraged. Political scientist Andrew Hacker of Queens College lambastes[2] a task-force suggestion that children be taught how "Native Americans were here to welcome new settlers form Holland, Senegal, England, Indonesia, France, the Congo, Italy, China, Iberia." Asks Hacker: "Did the Indians really welcome all those groups? Were they at Ellis Island when the Italians started to arrive? This is not history but a myth intended to bolster the self-esteem of certain children and, just possibly, a platform for advocates of various ethnic interests."

VALUES: SOMETHING IN COMMON

Economic and political issues, however much emotion they arouse, are fundamentally open to practical solution. The deeper significance of America's becoming a majority non-white society is what it means to the national psyche to individuals' sense of themselves and their nation — their idea of what it is to be American. People of color have often felt that whites treated equality as a benevolence granted to minorities rather than as an inherent natural right. Surely that condescension will wither.

Rather than accepting U.S. history and its meaning as settled, citizens will feel ever more free to debate where the nation's successes sprang from and what its unalterable beliefs are. They will clash over which myths and icons to invoke in education, in popular culture, in ceremonial speechmaking from political campaigns to the State of the Union address. Which is the more

1. Vituperative remarks are full of hate, anger, or insults.
2. If you lambast someone, you criticize them severely, usually in public.

admirable heroism: the courageous holdout by a few conquest-minded whites over Hispanics at the Alamo, or the anonymous expression of hope by millions who filed through Ellis Island? Was the subduing of the West a daring feat of bravery and ingenuity, or a wretched example of white imperialism? Symbols deeply meaningful to one group can be a matter of indifference to another. Says University of Wisconsin chancellor Donna Shalala: "My grandparents came from Lebanon. I don't identify with the Pilgrims on a personal level." Christopher, Jencks, professor of sociology at Northwestern, asks, "Is anything more basic about turkeys and pilgrims than about Martin Luther King and Selma? To me, it's six of one and half a dozen of the other, if children understand what it's like to be a dissident minority. Because the civil rights struggle is closer chronologically, it's likelier to be taught by someone who really cares."

Traditionalists increasingly distinguish between a "multi-racial" society, which they say would be fine, and a "multi-cultural" society, which they deplore. They argue that every society needs a universally accepted set of values and that new arrivals should therefore be pressured to conform to the mentality on which U.S. prosperity and freedom were built. Says Allan Bloom, author of the best-selling *The Closing of the American Mind*: "Obviously, the future of America can't be sustained if people keep only to their own ways and remain perpetual outsiders. The society has got to turn them into Americans. There are natural fears that today's immigrants may be too much of a cultural stretch for a nation based on Western values."

The counterargument, made by such scholars as historian Thomas Bender of New York University, is that if the center cannot hold, then one must redefine the center. It should be, he says, "the ever changing outcome of a continuing contest among social groups and ideas for the power to define public culture." Besides, he adds, many immigrants arrive committed to U.S. values; that is part of what attracted them. Says Julian Simon, professor of business administration at the University of Maryland: "The life and institutions here shape immigrants and not vice versa. This business about immigrants changing our institutions and our basic ways of life is hogwash[1]. It's nativist scare talk."

CITIZENSHIP: FORGING A NEW IDENTITY

Historians note that Americans have felt before that their historical culture was being overwhelmed by immigrants, but conflicts between earlier-arriving English, Germans and Irish and later-arriving Italians and Jews did not have the obvious and enduring element of racial skin color. And there was never a time when the nonmainstream element could claim, through sheer numbers, the potential to unite and exert political dominance. Says Bender: "The real question is whether or not our notion of diversity can successfully negotiate the color line."

For whites, especially those who trace their ancestry back to the early years of the Republic, the American heritage is a source of pride. For people of color, it is more likely to evoke anger and sometimes shame. The place where hope is shared is in the future. Demographer Ben Wattenberg, formerly perceived as a resister to social change, says "There's a nice chance that the American myth in the 1990s and beyond is going to ratchet another step toward this idea that we are the universal nation. That rings the bell of manifest destiny. We're a people with a mission and a sense of purpose, and we believe we have something to offer the world."

Not every erstwhile alarmist can bring himself to such optimism. Says Norman Podhoretz, editor of *Commentary*: "A lot of people are trying to undermine the foundations of the American experience and are pushing toward a more Balkanized society. I think that would be a disaster, not only because it would destroy a precious social inheritance but also because it would lead to enormous unrest, even violence."

While know-nothingism is generally confined to the more dismal corners of the American psyche, it seems all too predictable that during the next decades many more mainstream white Americans will begin to speak openly about the nation they feel they are losing. There are not, after all, many nonwhite faces

1. If you describe what someone says as hogwash, you think it is nonsense

depicted in Norman Rockwell's painting. White Americans are accustomed to thinking of themselves as the very picture of their nation. Inspiring as it may be to the rest of the world, significant as it may be to the U.S. role in global politics, world trade and the pursuit of peace, becoming a conspicuously multiracial society is bound to be a somewhat bumpy[1] experience for many ordinary citizens. For older Americans, raised in a world where the numbers of whites were greater and the visibility of nonwhites was carefully restrained, the new world will seem ever stranger. But as children in . . . classrooms across the nation are coming to realize, the new world is here. It is now. And it is irreversibly the America to come.

1. A bumpy journey is uncomfortable and rough, usually because you are travelling over an uneven surface.

AFTER YOU READ

1. By 2056, when someone born today will be 66 years old, … According to the above sentence, when is today?

2. This process has been one of country's great strengths. Would you explain this process?

3. Which language do many Hispanics now seek to use?

4. Why are blacks uneasy about being supplanted by other minorities?

5. What are white Americans accustomed to ?

6. Children in classroom across the nation are coming to realize, the new world is here. What is the new world?

12

FIFTH AVENUE, UPTOWN: A LETTER FROM HALERM

James Baldwin (1924-1987)

one of the great African American writers; his essays and fiction reveal his intense interest in social concerns. Long an expatriate, Baldwin's early experiences, both as a preacher's son and as a preacher himself, contribute to the powerful rhythm of his prose. In this writing, Baldwin describes the dehumanizing effects of ghetto life in Harlem.

There is a housing project standing now where the house in which we grew up once stood, and one of those stunted city trees is snarling where our doorway used to be. This is on the rehabilitated side of the avenue. The other side of the avenue—for progress takes time—has not been rehabilitated yet and it looks exactly as it looked in the days when we sat with our noses pressed against the windowpane, longing to be allowed to go "across the street." The grocery store which gave us credit is still there, and there can be no doubt that it is still giving credit. The people in the project certainly need it—far more, indeed, than they ever needed the project. The last time I passed by, the Jewish proprietor was still standing among his shelves, looking sadder and heavier but scarcely any older. Farther down the block stands the shoe-repair store in which our shoes were repaired until reparation became impossible and in which, then, we bought all our "new" ones. The Negro proprietor is still in the window, head down, working at the leather.

These two, I imagine, could tell a long tale if they would (perhaps they would be glad to if they could), having watched so many, for so long, struggling in the fishhooks, the barbed wire, of this avenue.

The avenue is elsewhere the renowned and elegant Fifth. The area I am describing, which, in today's gang parlance, would be called "the turf[1]," is bounded by Lenox Avenue on the west, the Harlem River on the east, 135th Street on the north, and 130th Street on the south. We never lived beyond these boundaries; this is where we grew up. Walking along 145th Street—for example—familiar as it is, and similar, does not have the same impact because I did not know any of the people on the block. But when I turn east on 131st Street and Lenox Avenue, there is first a soda-pop joint, then a shoeshine "parlor," then a grocery store, then a dry cleaners'. then the houses. All along the street there are people who watched me grow up, people who grew up with me, people I watched grow up along with my brothers and sisters: and, sometimes in my arms, sometimes underfoot, sometimes at my shoulder—or on it—their children, a riot, a forest of children, who include my nieces and nephews.

When we reach the end of this long block, we find ourselves on wide, filthy, hostile Fifth Avenue, facing that project which hangs over the avenue like a monument to the folly, and the cowardice, of good intentions. All along the block, for anyone who knows it, are immense human gaps, like craters. These gaps are not created merely by those who have moved away, inevitably into some other ghetto; or by those who have risen, almost always into a greater capacity for self-loathing and self-delusion; or yet by those who, by whatever means—War Ⅱ, the Korean war, a policeman's gun or billy, a gang war, a brawl, madness, an overdose of heroin, or, simply, unnatural exhaustion—are dead. I am talking about those who are left. and I am talking principally about the young. What are they doing? Well, some, a minority are fanatical churchgoers, members of the more extreme of the Holy Roller sects. Many, many more are "moslems," by affiliation or sympathy, that is to say that they are united by nothing more—and nothing less—than a hatred of the white world and all its works. They are present, for example, at every Buy Black street-corner meeting— meetings in which the speaker urges his hearers to cease trading with white men and establish a separate economy.

---

1. Someone's turf is the area which is most familiar to them or where they feel most confidant. (=territory)

Neither the speaker nor his hearers can possibly do this, of course, since Negroes do not own General Motors or RCA or the A&P, nor, indeed, do they own more than a wholly insufficient fraction of anything else in Harlem (those who *do* own anything are more interested in their profits than in their fellows). But these meetings nevertheless keep alive in the participators a certain pride of bitterness without which, however futile this bitterness may be, they could scarcely remain alive at all. Many have given up. They stay home and watch the TV screen, living on the earnings of their parents, cousins, brothers, or uncles, and only leave the house to go to the movies or to the nearest bar. "How're you making it?" one may ask, running into them along the block, or in the bar. "Oh, I'm TVing it", with the saddest, sweetest, most (shame-faced of smiles, and from a great distance. This distance one is compelled to respect; anyone who has traveled so far will not easily be dragged again into the world. There are further retreats, of course, than the TV screen or the bar. There are those who are simply sitting on their stoops, "stoned[1]," animated for a moment only, and hideously, by the approach of someone who may lend them the money for a "fix." Or by the approach of someone from whom they can purchase it, one of the shrewd ones, on the way to prison or just coming out.

And the others, who have avoided all of these deaths, get up in the morning and go downtown to meet "the man." The work in the white man's world all day and come home in the evening to this fetid block. They struggle to instill in their children some private sense of honor or dignity which will help the child survive. This means, of course, that they must struggle, stolidly, incessantly, to keep this sense alive in themselves, in spite of the insults, the indifference, and the cruelty they are certain to encounter in their working day. They patiently browbeat the landlord into fixing the heat, the plaster, the plumbing; this demands prodigious patience, nor is patience usually enough. In trying to make their hovels habitable, they are perpetually throwing good money after bad. Such frustration, so long endured, is driving many strong, admirable men and women whose only crime is color to the very

1. If someone is stoned, their mind is greatly affected by a drug such as cannabis

gates of paranoia.

One remembers them from another time—playing handball in the playground, going to church, wondering if they were going to be promoted at school. One remembers them going off to war—gladly, to escape this block. One remembers their return. Perhaps one remembers their wedding day. And one sees where the girl is now—vainly looking for salvation from some other embittered, trussed[1], and struggling boy—and sees the all-but-abandoned children in the streets.

Now I am perfectly aware that there are other slums in which white men are fighting for their lives, and mainly losing. I know that blood is also flowing through those streets and that the human damage there is incalculable. People are continually pointing out to me the wretchedness of white people in order to console me for the wretchedness of blacks. But an itemized account of the American failure does not console me and it should not console anyone else. That hundreds of thousands of white people are living, in effect, no better than the "niggers" is not a fact to be regarded with complacency. The social and moral bankruptcy suggested by this fact is of the bitterest, most terrifying kind.

The people, however, who believe that this democratic anguish has some consoling value are always pointing out that So-and-So, white, and So-and-So, black, rose from the slums into the big time.[2] The existence—the public existence—of, say, Frank Sinatra and Sammy Davis, Jr. proves to them that America is still the land of opportunity and that inequalities vanish before the determined will. It proves nothing of the sort. The determined will is rare—at the moment, in this country, it is unspeakably rare—and the inequalities suffered by the many are in no way justified by the rise of a few. A few have always risen—in every country, every era, and in the teeth of[3] regimes which can by

1. To truss someone means to tie them up very tightly so that they cannot move. (=bind)
2. You can use big time to refer to the highest level of an activity or sport where you can achieve the greatest amount of success or importance. If you describe a person as big time, you mean they are successful and important.
3. If you do something in the teeth of a difficulty or danger, you do it in spite of the difficulty or danger.

no stretch of the imagination be thought of as free. Not all of these people, it is worth remembering, left the world better than they found it. The determined will is rare, but it is not invariably benevolent. Furthermore, the American equation of success with the big times reveals an awful disrespect for human life and human achievement. This equation has placed our cities among the most dangerous in the world and has placed our youth among the most empty and most bewildered. The situation of our youth is not mysterious. Children have never been very good at listening to their elders, but they have never failed to imitate them. They must, they have no other models. That is exactly what our children are doing. They are imitating our immortality, our disrespect for the pain of others.

All other slum dwellers, when the bank account permits it, can move out of the slum and vanish altogether from the eye of persecution. No Negro in this country has ever made that much money and it will be a long time before any Negro does. The Negroes in Harlem, who have no money, spend what they have on such gimcracks as they are sold. These include "wider" TV screens, more "faithful" hi-fi sets, more "powerful" cars, all of which, of course, are obsolete long before they are paid for. Anyone who has ever struggled with poverty knows how extremely expensive it is to be poor; and if one is a member of a captive population, economically speaking, one's feet have placed on the treadmill forever. One is victimized, economically, in a thousand ways—rent, for example, or car insurance. Go shopping one day in Harlem—for anything—and compare Harlem prices and quality with those downtown.

The people who have managed to get off this block have only got as far as a more respectable ghetto. This respectable ghetto does not even have the advantages of the disreputable one—friends, neighbors, a familiar church, and friendly tradesmen; and it is not, moreover, in the nature of[1] any ghetto to remain respectable long. Every Sunday, people who have left the block take the lonely ride back, dragging their increasingly discontented children with them. They spend the day talking, not always with

1. If you say that one thing is in the nature of another. you mean that it is like the other thing.

words, about the trouble they've seen and the trouble—one must watch their eyes as they watch their children—they are only too likely to see. For children do not like ghettos. It takes them nearly no time to discover exactly why they are there.

The projects in Harlem are hated. They are hated almost as much as policemen, and this is saying a great deal. And they are hated for the same reason: both reveal, unbearably, the real attitude of the white world, no matter how many liberal speeches are made, no matter how many lofty editorials are written, no matter how many civil-rights commissions are set up.

The projects are hideous, of course, there being a law, apparently respected throughout the world, that popular housing shall be as cheerless as a prison. They are jumped all over Harlem, colorless, bleak, high, and revolting. The wide windows look out on Harlem's invincible and indescribable squalor: the Park Avenue railroad tracks, around which, about forty years ago, the present dark community began: the unrehabilitated houses, bowed down, it would seem, under the great weight of the frustration and bitterness they contain; the dark, the ominous schoolhouses from which the child may emerge maimed, blinded, hooked, or engaged for life: and the churches, churches, block upon block of churches, niched in the walls like cannon in the walls of a fortress. Even if the administration of the projects were not so insanely humiliating (for example: one must report raises in salary to the management, which will then eat up the profit by raising one's rent: the management has the right to know who is staying in your apartment: the management can ask you to leave, at their discretion), the projects would still be hated because they are an insult to the meanest intelligence.

Harlem got its first private project, Riverton—which is now, naturally, a slum—about twelve years ago because at that time Negroes were not allowed to live in Stuyvesant Town. Harlem watched Riverton go up, therefore in the most violent bitterness of spirit, and hated it long before the builders arrived. They began hating it at about the time people began moving out of their condemned houses to make room for this additional proof of how thoroughly the white world despised them. And They had scarcely moved in, naturally, before they began smashing windows, defacing walls, urinating in the elevators, and fornicating[1] in the playgrounds. Liberals, both white and black, were appalled at the spectacle. I was appalled by the liberal innocence—or cynicism, which comes out in practice as much the same thing. Other people were delighted to be able to point to proof positive that nothing could be done to better the lot of the colored people. They were, and are, right in one respect: that nothing con be done as long as they are treated like colored people. The people in Harlem know they are living there because white people do not think they are good enough to live anywhere else. No amount of "improvement" can sweeten this fact. Whatever money is now being earmarked[2] to improve this, or any other ghetto, might as well be burnt. A ghetto can be improved in one way only: out of existence.

Similarly, the only way to police a ghetto is to be oppressive. None of the Police Commissioner's men, even with the best will in the world, have any way of understanding the lives led by the people they swagger about in twos and threes controlling. Their very presence is an insult, and it would be, even if they spent their entire day feeding gumdrops to children. They represent the force of the white world, and the world's real intentions are, simply for the world's criminal profit and ease, to keep the black man corralled up here, in his place. The badge, the gun in the holster, and the swinging club make vivid what will happen should his rebellion become overt. Rare, indeed, is the Harlem citizen, from the most circumspect[3] church member to the most shiftless adolescent, who does not have a long tale to tell of police incompetence, injustice, or brutality. I myself have witnessed and endured it more than once. The businessmen and racketeers also have a story. And so do the prostitutes. (And this is not, perhaps, the place to discuss Harlem's very complex attitude toward black policemen, nor the reasons, according to Harlem, that they are nearly all downtown.)

It is hard, on the other hand, to blame the policeman, blank,

1. To fornicate means to have sex with someone you are not married to.
2. If resources such as money are earmarked for a particular purpose, they are reserved for that purpose. (=set aside)
3. If you are circumspect, you are cautious in what you do and say and do not take risks. (=cautious, careful)

good-natured, thoughtless, and insuperably innocent, for being such a perfect representative of the people he serves. He, too, believes in good intentions and is astounded and offended when they are not taken for the deed. He has never, himself, done anything for which to be hated—which of us has?—and yet he is facing, daily and nightly, people who would gladly see him dead, and he knows it. There is no way for him not to know it: there are few things under heaven more unnerving[1] than the silent, accumulating contempt and hatred of a people. He moves through Harlem, therefore, like an occupying soldier in a bitterly hostile country; which is precisely what, and where, he is, and is the reason he walks in twos and threes. And he is not the only one who knows why he is always in company: the people who are watching him know why, too. Any street meeting, sacred or secular, which he and his colleagues uneasily cover has as its explicit or implicit burden the cruelty and injustice of the white domination. And these days, of course, in terms increasingly vivid and jubilant, it speaks of the end of that domination. The white policeman standing on a Harlem street corner finds himself at the very center of the revolution now occurring in the world. He is not prepared for it—naturally, nobody is—and, what is possibly much more to the point, he is exposed, as few white people are, to the anguish of the black people around him. Even if he is gifted with the merest mustard grain of imagination, something must seep in. He cannot avoid observing that some of the children, in spite of their color, remind him of children he has known and loved, perhaps even of his own children. He knows that he certainly does not want his children living this way. He can retreat from his uneasiness in only one direction: into a callousness which very shortly becomes second nature. He becomes more callous, the population becomes more hostile, the situation grows more tense, and the police force is increased. One day, to everyone's astonishment, someone drops a match in the powder keg and everything blows up. Before the dust has settled or the blood congealed, editorials, speeches, and civil-rights commissions are loud in the land, demanding to know what

---

1. If you describe something as unnerving, you mean that it makes you feel worried or uncomfortable. (=disconcerting)

happened. What happened is that Negroes wants to be treated like men.

Negroes want to be treated like men: a perfectly straightforward statement, containing only seven words. People who have mastered Kant, Hegel, Shakespeare, Marx, Freud, and the Bible find this statement utterly impenetrable[1]. The idea seems to threaten profound, barely conscious assumptions. A kind of panic paralyzes their features, as though they found themselves trapped on the edge of a steep place. I once tried to describe to a very well-known American intellectual the conditions among Negroes in the South. My recital disturbed him and made him indignant; and he asked me in perfect innocence, "Why don't all the Negroes in the South move North?" I tried to explain what *has* happened, unfailingly, whenever a significant body of Negroes move North. They do not escape Jim Crow: they merely encounter another, not-less-deadly variety. They do not move to Chicago, they move to the South Side; they do not move to New York, they move to Harlem. The pressure within the ghetto causes the ghetto walls to expand, and this expansion is always violent. White people hold the line as long as they can, and in as many ways as they can, from verbal intimidation to physical violence. But inevitably the border which has divided the ghetto from the rest of the world falls into the hands of the ghetto. The white people fall back bitterly before the black horde; the landlords make a tidy profit by raising the rent, chopping up the rooms, and all but dispensing with the upkeep; and what has once been a neighborhood turns into a "turf." This is precisely what happened when the Puerto Ricans arrived in their thousands—and the bitterness thus caused is, as I write, being fought out all up and down those streets.

Northerners indulge in an extremely dangerous luxury. They seem to feel that because they fought on the right side during the Civil War, and won, they have earned the right merely to deplore what is going on in the South, without taking any responsibility for it; and that they can ignore what is happening in Northern cities because what is happening in Little Rock or Birmingham

1. If you describe something such as a book or a theory as impenetrable, you are emphasizing that it is impossible or very difficult to understand. (=incomprehensible)

is worse. Well, in the first place, it is not possible for anyone who has not endured both to know which is "worse." I know Negroes who prefer the South and white Southerners, because "At least there, you haven't got to play any guessing games!" The guessing games referred to have driven more than one Negro into the narcotics ward, the madhouse, or the river. I know another Negro, a man very dear to me, who says with conviction and with truth, "The spirit of the South is the spirit of America." He was born in the North and did his military training in the South. He did not, as far as I can gather, find the South "worse", he found it, if anything, all too familiar. In the second place, though, even if Birmingham is worse, no doubt Johannesburg, South Africa, beats it by several miles, and Buchenwald was one of the worst things that ever happened in the entire history of the world. The world has never lacked for horrifying examples; but I do not believe that these examples are meant to be used as justification for our own crimes. This perpetual justification empties the heart of all human feeling. The emptier our hearts become, the greater will be our crimes. Thirdly, the South is not merely an embarrassingly backward region, but a part of this country, and what happens there concerns everyone of us.

As far as the color problem is concerned, there is but one difference between the Southern white and the Northerner: the Southerner remembers, historically and in his own psyche, a kind of Eden in which he loved black people and they loved him. Historically, the flaming sword laid across this Eden is the Civil War. Personally, it is the Southerner's sexual coming of age, when, without any warning, unbreakable taboos are set up between himself and his past. Everything, thereafter, is permitted him except the love he remembers and has never ceased to need. The resulting, indescribable torment affects every Southern mind and is the basis of the Southern hysteria.

None of this is true for the Northerner. Negroes represent nothing to him personally, except, perhaps, the dangers of carnality. He never sees Negroes. Southerners see them all the time. Northerners never think about them whereas Southerners are never really thinking of anything else. Negroes are, therefore, ignored in the North and are under surveillance in the south, and suffer hideously[1] in both places. Neither the Southerner nor the Northerner is able to look on the Negro simply as a man. It seems to be indispensable to the national self-esteem that the Negro be considered either as a kind of ward (in which case we are told how many Negroes, comparatively, bought Cadillac last year and how few, comparatively, were lynched), or as a victim (in which case we are promised that he will never vote in our assemblies or go to school with our kids). They are two sides of the same coin and the South will not change—*cannot* change—until the North changes. The country will not change until it re-examines itself and discovers what it really means by freedom. In the meantime, generations keep being born, bitterness is increased by incompetence, pride, and folly, and the world shrinks around us.

It is a terrible, an inexorable, law that one cannot deny the humanity of another without diminishing one's own: in the face of one's victim, one sees oneself. Walk through the streets of Harlem and see what we, this nation, have become.

1. You can use hideous to emphasize that something is very unpleasant or unacceptable.

AFTER YOU READ

1. Where is exactly Harlem located in New York?

2. What does the American equation of success with the big times reveal?

3. How long will it take before any Negro move out of the slum?

4. Every Sunday where do people who have left the block spend the day?

5. Why does the Harlem citizen have a long tale to tell of the police?

6. What doe the writer think about the South?

13

MARTIN LUTHER KING JR.:
ADDRESS AT MARCH ON WASHINGTON FOR JOBS AND FREEDOM

I HAVE A DREAM

Martin Luther King Jr.[1]
Delivered on the steps at the Lincoln Memorial
in Washington D.C. on August 28, 1963.

I am happy to join with you today in what will go down[2] in history as the greatest demonstration for freedom in the history of our nation..

Five score years ago, a great American, in whose symbolic shadow we stand today, signed the Emancipation Proclamation. This momentous decree came as a great beacon light of hope to millions of Negro slaves, who had been seared in the flames of withering injustice. It came as a joyous daybreak to end the long night of captivity. But one hundred years later, the Negro is still not free. One hundred years later, the life of the Negro is still sadly crippled by the manacles[3] of segregation and the chains of discrimination.

One hundred years later, the Negro lives on a lonely island of poverty in the midst of a vast ocean of material prosperity. One hundred years later, the Negro is still languished[4] in the corners of American society and finds himself an exile in his own land. So we've come here today to dramatize a shameful condition.

In a sense we have come to our nation's capital to cash a

1. Martin Luther King Jr. (1929~68): 미국 침례교파의 흑인 목사; 차별 철폐, 평화 운동 지도자; Nobel 평화상 수상(1964)
2. go down: be recorded in writing
3. manacles: handcuff
4. languish: lose or lack vitality

check. When the architects of our republic wrote the magnificent words of the Constitution and the Declaration of Independence, they were signing a promissory note to which every American was to fall heir.

This note was a promise that all men, yes, black men as well as white men, would be guaranteed the inalienable rights of life, liberty and the pursuit of happiness.

It is obvious today that America has defaulted[1] on this promissory note insofar as her citizens of color are concerned. Instead of honoring this sacred obligation, America has given the Negro people a bad check, a check which has come back marked "insufficient funds."

But we refuse to believe that the bank of justice is bankrupt. We refuse to believe that there are insufficient funds in the great vaults[2] of opportunity of this nation. So we have come to cash this check, a check that will give us upon demand the riches of freedom and the security of justice.

We have also come to this hallowed[3] spot to remind America of the fierce urgency of Now. This is no time to engage in the luxury of cooling off or to take the tranquilizing drug of gradualism. Now is the time to make real the promises of democracy. Now is the time to rise from the dark and desolate valley of segregation to the sunlit path of racial justice. Now is the time to lift our nation from the quicksands[4] of racial injustice to the solid rock of brotherhood. Now is the time to make justice a reality for all of God's children.

It would be fatal for the nation to overlook the urgency of the moment. This sweltering summer of the Negro's legitimate discontent will not pass until there is an invigorating autumn of freedom and equality. Nineteen sixty-three is not an end but a beginning. Those who hope that the Negro needed to blow off steam and will now be content will have a rude awakening if the nation returns to business as usual.

There will be neither rest nor tranquility in America until the

1. default: fail to fulfil(esp. a legal) obligation
2. vault: a secure room where money and other valuable things can be kept safely
3. hallow: make holy, consecrate
4. quicksand: area of loose wet sand that sucks in anything placed on it

Negro is granted his citizenship rights. The whirlwinds of revolt will continue to shake the foundations of our nation until the bright day of justice emerges.

But there is something that I must say to my people who stand on the warm threshold which leads into the palace of justice. In the process of gaining our rightful place we must not be guilty of wrongful deeds.

Let us not seek to satisfy our thirst for freedom by drinking from the cup of bitterness and hatred. We must ever conduct our struggle on the high plane of dignity and discipline. We must not allow our creative protest to degenerate into physical violence. Again and again we must rise to the majestic heights of meeting physical force with soul force.

The marvelous new militancy which has engulfed the Negro community must not lead us to a distrust of all white people, for many of our white brothers, as evidenced by their presence here today, have come to realize that their destiny is tied up with our destiny. They have come to realize that their freedom is inextricably bound to our freedom. We cannot walk alone.

And as we walk, we must make the pledge that we shall always march ahead. We cannot turn back. There are those who are asking the devotees of civil rights. "When will you be satisfied?" We can never be satisfied as long as the Negro is the victim of the unspeakable horrors of police brutality.

We can never be satisfied as long as our bodies, heavy with the fatigue of travel, cannot gain lodging in the motels of the highways and the hotels of the cities. We cannot be satisfied as long as a negro in Mississippi cannot vote and a Negro in New York believes he has nothing for which to vote.

No, no, we are not satisfied, and we will not be satisfied, and we will not be satisfied until justice rolls down like waters and righteousness like a mighty stream.

I am not unmindful that some of you have come here out of great trials and tribulations[1]. Some of you have come fresh from narrow jail cells. Some of you have come from areas where your quest for freedom left you battered by the storms of persecutions and staggered by the winds of police brutality. You have been the

1. tribulation: great affliction

veterans of creative suffering. Continue to work with the faith that unearned suffering is redemptive.

Go back to Mississippi, go back to Alabama, go back to South Carolina, go back to Georgia, go back to Louisiana, go back to the slums and ghettos of our northern cities, knowing that somehow this situation can and will be changed.

Let us not wallow[1] in the valley of despair. I say to you today, my friends, that even though we face the difficulties of today and tomorrow, I still have a dream. It is a dream deeply rooted in the American dream.

I have a dream that one day this nation will rise up and live out the true meaning of its creed—we hold these truths to be self-evident that all men are created equal.

I have a dream that one day on the red hills of Georgia the sons of former slaves and the sons of former slave owners will be able to sit down together at a table of brotherhood.

I have a dream that one day even the state of Mississippi, a state sweltering with the heat of injustice, sweltering with the heat of oppression, will be transformed into an oasis of freedom and justice.

I have a dream that my four little children will one day live in a nation where they will not be judged by the color of their skin but by the content of their character.

I have a dream today!

I have a dream that one day, down in Alabama, with its vicious racists, with its governor having his lips dripping with the words of interposition[2] and nullification[3]; one day right down in Alabama little black boys and black girls will be able to join hands with little white boys and white girls as sisters and brothers.

I have a dream today!

I have a dream that one day every valley shall be exalted, every hill and mountain shall be made low, the rough places will be made plain, and the crooked places will be made straight and the glory of the Lord shall be revealed and all flesh shall see it together.

---

1. wallow: flounder about
2. interposition: (미) 각 주는 그 주권을 침해하는 것으로 간주되는 연방정부의 조치에 반대할 수 있다는 주의.
3. nullification: (미) 주내에서의 연방법의 실시 거부

This is our hope. This is the faith that I will go back to the South with. With this faith we will be able to hew[1] out of the mountain of despair a stone of hope. With this faith we will be able to transform the jangling discords of our nation into a beautiful symphony of brotherhood. With this faith we will be able to work together, to pray together, to struggle together, to go to jail together, to stand up for freedom together, knowing that we will be free one day. This will be the day, this will be the day when all of God's children will be able to sing with a new meaning, "My country, 'tis of thee, sweet land of liberty, of thee I sing. Land where my fathers died, land of the Pilgrim's pride, from every mountainside, let freedom ring!" And if America is to be a great nation this must become true.

And so let freedom ring from the prodigious hilltops of New Hampshire.

Let freedom ring from the mighty mountains of New York.

Let freedom ring from the heightening Alleghenies of Pennsylvania.

Let freedom ring from the snow-capped Rockies of Colorado.

Let freedom ring from the curvaceous slopes of California.

But not only that.

Let freedom ring from Stone Mountain of Georgia.

Let freedom ring from Lookout Mountain of Tennessee.

Let freedom ring from every hill and molehill of Mississippi, from every mountainside, let freedom ring!

And when this happens, when we allow freedom to ring, when we let it ring from every tenement and every hamlet, from every state and every city, we will be able to speed up that day when all of God's children, black men and white men, Jews and Gentiles[2], Protestants and Catholics, will be able to join hands and sing in the words of the old Negro spiritual, "Free at last, free at last. Thank God Almighty, we are free at last."

---

1. hew: chop or cut with an axe, sword, etc.
2. Gentiles: <,유대인의 입장에서 본> 이방인

AFTER YOU READ

1. Why did black people gather at the Lincoln Memorial in Washington D. C.?

2. America has given the Negro people a bad check. What does that mean?

3. They have come to cash this check. What kind of check is this?

4. When will black people satisfy?

5. Which states especially have bad reputations for discrimination and segregation?

14

HOME IS WHERE THE HAN IS:

A KOREAN-AMERICAN PERSPECTIVE ON THE LOS ANGELES UPHEAVALS

Elaine H. Kim

Elaime H. Kim teaches Asian American Studies at the University of California — Berkeley. She has written and edited a number of books on Asian American writers and artists, and she has been involved in the production of television documentaries on Asian women. The following selection originally appeared as a chapter in a collection of essays, *Reading Rodney King/ Reading Urban Uprising* (1993)

About half of the estimated $850 million in estimated material losses incurred during the Los Angles upheavals was sustained[1] by a community no one seems to want to talk much about. Korean American in Los Angeles, suddenly at the front lines when violence came to the buffer zone they had been so precariously occupying, suffered profound damage to their means of livelihood. But my concern here is the psychic damage which, unlike material damage, is impossible to quantify.

I want to explore the questions of whether or not recovery is possible for Korean Americans, and what will become of our attempts to "become American" without dying of *han*. *Han* is a Korean word that means, loosely translated, the sorrow and anger that grow from the accumulated experiences of oppression. Although the word is frequently and commonly used by Koreans, the condition it describes is taken quite seriously. When people die of *han*, it is called dying of *hwabyong*, a disease of frustration and rage following misfortune.

Situated as we are on the border between those who have and those who have not, between predominantly Anglo and mostly

1. If you sustain something such as a defeat, loss, or injury, it happens to you.

African American and Latino communities, from our current interstitial position in the American discourse of race, many Korean Americans have trouble calling what happened in Los Angeles an "uprising." At the same time, we cannot quite say it was a "riot." So some of us have taken to calling it *sa-i-ku*, April 29, after the manner of naming other events in Korean history —3.1 (*sam-il*) for March 1, 1919, when massive protests against Japanese colonial rule began in Korea; 6.25 (*yook-i-o*), or June 25, 1950, when the Korean War began; and 4.19 (*sa-il-ku*), or April 19, 1960, when the first student movement in the world to overthrow a government began in South Korea. The ironic similarity between 4.19 and 4.29 does not escape most Korean Americans.

Los Angeles Koreatown has been important to me, even though I visit only a dozen times a year. Before Koreatown sprang up during the last decade and a half, I used to hang around[1] the fringes of Chinatown, although I knew that this habit was pure pretense. For me, knowing that Los Angeles Koreatown existed made a difference[2]; one of my closest friends worked with the Black-Korean Alliance there, and I liked to think of it as a kind of "home":—however idealized and hypostatized—for the soul, an anchor, a potential refuge, a place in America where I could belong without ever being asked, "Who are you and what are you doing here? Where did you come from and when are you going back?"

Many of us watched in horror the destruction of Koreatown and the systematic targeting of Korean shops in South Central Los Angeles after the Rodney King verdict. Seeing those buildings in flames and those anguished Korean faces, I had the terrible thought that there would be no belonging and that we were, just as I had always suspected, a people destined to carry our *han* around with us wherever we went in the world. The destiny (*p'aljja*) that had spelled centuries of extreme suffering from invasion, colonization, war, and national division had smuggled

1. If you hang around, hang about, or hang round with someone or in a particular place, you spend a lot of time with that person or in that place.
2. If something makes a difference or makes a lot of difference, it affects you and helps you in what you are doing. If something makes no difference, it does not have any effect what you are doing. *Where you live can make such a difference to the way you feel.

itself into the U.S. with our baggage.

AFRICAN AMERICAN AND KOREAN AMERICAN CONFLICT

As someone whose social consciousness was shaped by the African American-led civil rights movement of the 1960s, I felt that I was watching our collective dreams for a just society disintegrating, cast aside as naive and irrelevant in the bitter and embattled 1990s. It was the courageous African American women and men of the 1960s who had redefined the meaning of "American," who had first suggested that a person like me could reject the false choice between being treated as a perpetual foreigner in my own birthplace, on the one hand, and relinquishing[1] my identity for someone else's ill-fitting and impossible Anglo American one on the other. Thanks to them, I began to discern how institutional racism works and why Korea was never mentioned in my world-history textbooks. I was able to see how others besides Koreans had been swept aside by the dominant culture. My American education offered nothing about Chicanos or Latinos, and most of what I was taught about African and Native Americans was distorted to justify their oppression and vindicate their oppressors.

I could hardly believe my ears when, during the weeks immediately following *sa-i-ku*, I heard African American community leaders suggesting that Korean American merchants were foreign intruders deliberately trying to stifle African American economic development, when I knew that they had bought those liquor stores at five times gross receipts from African American owners, who had previously bought them at two times gross receipts from Jewish owners after Watts. I saw anti-Korean flyers that were being circulated by African American political candidates and read about South Central residents petitioning against the reestablishment of swap meets, groups of typically Korean immigrant-operated market stalls. I was disheartened with Latinos who related the pleasure they felt while looting Korean stores that they believed "had it coming" and who claimed that it

1. If you relinquish such as power or control, you give it up.

was because of racism that more Latinos were arrested during *sa-i-ku* than Asian Americans. And I was filled with despair when I read about Chinese Americans wanting to dissociate themselves from us. According to one Chinese American reporter assigned to cover Asian American issues for a San Francisco daily, Chinese and Japanese American shopkeepers, unlike Koreans, always got along fine with African Americans in the past. "Suddenly," admitted another Chinese American, "I am scared to be Asian. More specifically, I am afraid to be mistaken for Korean." I was enraged when I overheard European Americans discussing the conflicts as if they were watching a dogfight or a boxing match. The situation reminded me of the Chinese film "Raise the Red Lantern," in which we nerver see the husband's face. We only hear his mellifluous voice as he benignly admonishes his four wives not to fight among themselves. He can afford to be kind and pleasant because the structure that pits[1] his wives against each other is so firmly in place that he need never sully his hands or even raise his voice.

BATTLEGROUND LEGACY

Korean Americans are squeezed between black and white and also between U.S. and South Korean political agendas. Opportunistic American and South Korean presidential candidates toured the burnt ruins, posing for the television cameras but delivering nothing of substance to the victims. Like their U.S. counterparts, South Korean news media seized upon *sa-i-ku*, featuring sensational stories that depicted the problem as that of savage African Americans attacking innocent Koreans for no reason. To give the appearance of authenticity, Seoul newspapers even published articles using the names of Korean Americans who did not in fact write them.

Those of us who chafe at being asked whether we are Chinese or Japanese as if there were no other possibilities or who were angered when the news media sought Chinese and Japanese but

1. If two opposing things or people are pitted against one another, they are in conflict.

not Korean American views during *sa-i-ku* are sensitive to an invisibility that seems particular to us. To many Americans, Korea is but the gateway to or the bridge between China and Japan, or a crossroads of major Asian conflicts.

It can certainly be said that, although little known or cared about in the Western world, Korea has been a perennial battleground. Besides the Mongols and the Manchus, there were the *Yŏjin* (Jurched), the *Koran* (Khitan), and the *Waega* (Wäkö) invaders. In relatively recent years, there was the war between China and Japan that ended in 1895 and the war between Japan and Russia in 1905; both of which were fought on Korean soil and resulted in extreme suffering for the Korean people. Japan's 36 years of brutal colonial rule ended with the U.S. and what was then the Soviet Union dividing the country in half at the 38th parallel. Thus, Korea was turned into a Cold War territory that ultimately became a battleground for world superpowers during the conflict of 1950-53.

BECOMING AMERICAN

One of the consequences of war, colonization, national division, and superpower economic and cultural domination has been the migration of Koreans to places like Los Angeles, where they believed their human rights would be protected by law. After all, they had received U.S.-influenced political educations. They started learning English in the seventh grade. They all knew the story of the poor boy from Illinois who became president. They all learned that the U.S. Constitution and Bill of Rights protected the common people from violence and injustice. But they who grew up in Korea watching "Gunsmoke," "Night Rider," and "McGyver" dubbed in Korean were not prepared for the black, brown, red, and yellow America they encountered when they disembarked at the Los Angeles International Airport. They hadn't heard that there is no equal justice in the U.S. They had to learn about American racial hierarchies. They did not realize that, as immigrants of color, they would never attain political voice or visibility but would instead be used to uphold the inequality and the racial hierarchy they had no part in creating.

Most of the newcomers had underestimated the communication barriers they would face. Like the Turkish workers in Germany described in John Berger and Jean Mohr's *A Seventh Man*, their toil amounted to only a pile of gestures and the English they tried to speak changed and turned against[1] them as they spoke it. Working 14 hours a day, six or seven days a week, they rarely came into sustained contact with English-speaking Americans and almost never had time to study English. Not feeling at ease with English, they did not engage in informal conversations easily with non-Koreans and were hated for being curt and rude. They did not attend churches or do business in bank or other enterprises where English was required. Typically, the immigrant, small-business owners utilized unpaid family labor instead of hiring people from local communities. Thanks to Eurocentric American cultural practices, they knew little or nothing good about African Americans or Latinos, who in turn and for similar reasons knew little or nothing good about them. At the same time, Korean shopowners in South Central and Koreatown were affluent compared with the impoverished residents, whom they often exploited as laborers or looked down upon as fools with an aversion to hard work. Most Korean immigrants did not even know that they were among the many direct beneficiaries of the African American-led civil rights movement, which helped pave the way for the 1965 immigration reforms that made their immigration possible.

Korean-immigrant views, shaped as they were by U.S. cultural influences and official, anticommunist, South Korean education, differed radically from those of many poor people in the communities Korea immigrants served: unaware of the shameful history of oppression of nonwhite immigrants and other people of color in the U.S., they regarded themselves as having arrived in a meritocratic "land of opportunity" where a person's chances for success are limited only by individual lack of ability or diligence. Having left a homeland where they foresaw their talents and hard work going unrecognized and unrewarded, they were desperate

1. If you turn against someone or something, or if you are turned against them, you stop supporting them, trusting them or liking them.

to believe that the "American dream" of social and economic mobility through hard work was within their reach.

SA-I-KU

What they experienced on 29 and 30 April was a baptism into what it really means for a Korean to "become American" in the 1990s. In South Korea, there is no 911, and no one really expects a fire engine or police car if there is trouble. Instead, people make arrangements with friends and family for emergencies. At the same time, guns are not part of Korean daily life. No civilian in South Korea can own a gun. Guns are the exclusive accoutrement of the military and police who enforce order for those who rule the society. When the Korean Americans in South Central and Koreatown dialed 911, nothing happened. When their stores and homes were being looted and burned to the ground, they were left completely alone for three horrifying days. How betrayed they must have felt by what they had believed was a democratic system that protects its people from violence. Those who trusted the government to protect them lost everything; those who took up arms after waiting for help for two days were able to defend themselves. It was as simple as that. What they had to learn was that, as in South Korea, protection in the U.S. is by and large for the rich and powerful. If there were a choice between Westwood and Koreatown, it is clear that Koreatown would have to be sacrificed. The familiar concept of privilege for the rich and powerful would have been easy for the Korean immigrant to grasp if only those exhortations about democracy and equality had not obfuscated[1] the picture. Perhaps they should have relied even more on whatever they brought with them from Korea instead of fretting over trying to understand what was going on around them here. That Koreatown became a battleground does seem like the further playing out of a tragic legacy that has followed them across oceans and continents. The difference is that this was a battle between the poor and disenfranchised and the invisible rich, who

1. To obfuscate something means to deliberately make it seem confusing and difficult to understand.

were being protected by a layer of clearly visible Korean American human shields in a battle on the buffer zone.

This difference is crucial. Perhaps the legacy is not one carried across oceans and continents but one assumed immediately upon arrival, not the curse of being Korean but the initiation into becoming American, which requires that Korean Americans take on[1] this country's legacy of five centuries of racial violence and inequality, of divide and rule, of privilege for the rich and oppression of the poor. Within this legacy, they have been assigned a place on the front lines. Silenced by those who possess the power to characterize and represent, they are permitted to speak only to reiterate their acceptance of this role.

SILENCING THE KORAN AMERICAN VOICE

Twelve years ago, in Kwangju, South Korea, hundreds of civilians demonstration for constitutional reform and free elections were murdered by U.S.-supported and -equipped South Korean elite paratroopers. Because I recorded it and played it over and over again, searching for a sign or a clue, I remember clearly how what were to me heartrendingly tragic events were represented in the U.S. news media. For a few fleeting moments, images of unruly crowds of alien-looking Asians shouting unintelligible words and phrases and wearing white headbands inscribed with unintelligible characters flickered across the screen The Koreans were made to seem like insane people from another planet. The voice in the background stated simply that there were massive demonstrations but did not explain what the protests were about. Nor was a single Korean ever given an opportunity to speak to the camera.

The next news story was about demonstrations for democracy in Poland. The camera settled on individuals' faces which one by one filled the screen as each man or woman was asked to explain how he or she felt. Each Polish person's words were translated in a voice-over or subtitle. Solidarity leader Lech Walesa, who was allowed to speak often, was characterized as a heroic human

1. If you take on a job or responsibility, especially a difficult one, you accept it.

being with whom all Americans could surely identify personally. Polish Americans from New York and Chicago to San Francisco, asked in man-on-the-street interviews about their reactions, described the canned hams and blankets they were sending to Warsaw.

This was for me a lesson in media representation, race, and power politics. It is a given that Americans are encouraged by our ideological apparatuses to side with our allies (here, the Polish resisters and the anti-communist South Korean government) against our enemies (here, the communist Soviet Union and protesters against the South Korean government). But visual-media racism helps craft and reinforce our identification with Europeans and whites while distancing us from fearsome and alien Asiatic hordes.

In March of last year, when two delegates from North Korea visited the Bay Area to participate in community-sponsored talks on Korean reunification, about 800 people form the Korean American community attended. The meeting was consummately newsworthy, since it was the first time in history that anyone from North Korea had ever been in California for more than 24 hours just passing through. The event was discussed for months in the Korean-language media—television, radio, and newspapers. Almost every Korean-speaking person in California knew about it. Although we sent press releases to all the commercial and public radio and television stations and to all the Bay Area newspapers, not a single mainstream media outfit[1] covered the event. However, whenever there was an African American boycott of a Korean store or whenever conflict surfaced between Korean and African Americans, community leaders found a dozen microphones from all the main news media shoved into their faces, as if they were the president's press secretary making an official public pronouncement. Fascination with interethnic conflicts is rooted in the desire to excuse or minimize white racism by buttressing the mistaken notion that all human beings are "naturally" racist, and when Korean and African Americans allow themselves to be distracted by these interests, their attention is deflected from the social hierarchies that give racism its destructive power.

1. You can refer to an organization as an outfit.

Without a doubt, the U.S. news media played a major role in exacerbating the damage and ill will toward Korean Americans, first by spotlighting tensions between African Americans and Koreans above all efforts to work together and as opposed to many other newsworthy events in these two communities, and second by exploiting racist stereotypes of Koreans as unfathomable aliens, this time wielding guns on rooftops and allegedly firing wildly into crowds. It news programs and on talk shows, African and Korean American tensions were discussed by blacks and whites, who pointed to these tensions as the main cause of the uprising. I heard some European Americans railing against rude and exploitative Korean merchants for ruining peaceful race relations for everyone else. Thus, Korean Americans were used to deflect attention from the racism they inherited and the economic injustice and poverty that had been already well wove into the fabric of American life, as evidenced by a judicial system that could allow not only the Korean store owner who killed Latasha Harlins but also the white men who killed Vincent Chin and the white police who beat Rodney King to go free, while Leonard Peltier still languishes in prison.

As far as I know, neither the commercial nor the public news media has mentioned the many Korean and African American attempts to improve relations, such as joint church services, joint musical performances and poetry readings, Korean merchant donations to African American community and youth programs, African American volunteer teachers in classes for Korean immigrants studying for citizenship examinations, or Korean translations of African American history materials.

While Koran immigrants were preoccupied with the mantra of day-to-day survival, Korean Americans had no voice, no political presence whatsoever in American life. When they became the targets of violence in Los Angeles, their opinions and views were hardly solicited[1] except as they could be used in the already-constructed mainstream discourse on race relations, which is a sorry combination of blaming the African American and Latino victims for their poverty and scapegoating the Korean Americans

1. If you solicit money, help, support, or an opinion from someone, you ask them for it.

as robotic aliens who have no "real" right to be here in the first place and therefore deserve whatever happens to them.

THE *NEWSWEEK* EXPERIENCE

In this situation, I felt compelled to respond when as editor from the "My Turn" section of *Newsweek* magazine asked for a 1000 word personal essay. Hesitant because I was given only a day and a half to write the piece, not enough time in light of the vastness of American ignorance about Koreans and Korean Americans, I decided to do it because I thought I could not be made into a sound bite[1] or a quote contextualized for someone else's agenda.

I wrote an essay accusing the news media of using Korean Americans and tensions between African and Korean Americans to divert attention from the roots of racial violence in the U.S. I asserted that these lie not in the Korean-immigrant-owned corner store situated in a community ravaged by poverty and police violence, but reach far back into the corridors of corporate and government offices in Los Angeles, Sacramento, and Washington, D.C. I suggested that Koreans and African Americans were kept ignorant about each other by educational and media institutions that erase or distort their experiences and perspectives. I tried to explain how racism had kept my parents from ever really becoming Americans, but that having been born here, I considered myself American and wanted to believe in the possibility of an American dream.

The editor of "My Turn" did everything he could to frame my words with his own viewpoint. He faxed his own introductory and concluding paragraphs that equated Korean merchants with cowboys in the Wild West and alluded to Korea/African American hatred. When I objected, he told me that my writing style was not crisp enough and that as an experienced Journalist, he could help me out. My confidence wavered, but ultimately I rejected his editing. Then he accused me of being overly sensitive,

1. A sound bite is a short sentence or phrase, usually from a politician's speech, which is broadcast during a news programme.

confiding that I had no need to be defensive—because his wife was a Chinese American. Only after I had decided to withdraw the piece did he agree to accept it as I wrote it.

Before I could finish congratulating myself on being able to resist silencing and the kind of decontextualization I was trying to describe in the piece, I started receiving hate mail. Some of it was addressed directly to me, since I had been identified as a University of California faculty member, but most of it arrived in bundles, forwarded by *Newsweek*. Hundreds of letters came from all over the country, from Florida to Washington state and from Massachusetts to Arizona. I was unprepared for the hostility expressed in most of the letters. Some people sent the article, torn from the magazine and covered with angry, red-inked obscenities scratched across my picture. "You should see a good doctor," wrote someone from Southern California, "you have severe problems in thinking, reasoning, and adjusting to your environment."

A significant proportion of the writers, especially those who identified themselves as descendants of immigrants from Eastern Europe, wrote *Newsweek* that they were outraged, sickened, disgusted, appalled, annoyed, and angry at the magazine for providing as arena for the paranoid, absurd, hypocritical, racist, and childish views of a spoiled, ungrateful, whining, bitching, un-American bogus faculty member who should be fired or die when the next California earthquake dumps all of the "so-called people of color" into the Pacific Ocean.

I was shocked by the profound ignorance of many writers' assumptions about the experiences and perspectives of American people of color in general and Korean and other Asian Americans in particular. Even though my essay revealed that I was born in the U.S. and that my parents had lived in the U.S. for more than six decades, I was viewed as a foreigner without the right to say anything except words of gratitude and praise about America. The letters also provided some evidence of the dilemma Korean Americans are placed in by those who assume that we are aliens who should "go back" and at the same time berate us for not rejecting "Korean-American identity" for "American identity."

How many Americans migrate to Korea? If you are so disenchanted, Korea is still there. Why did you ever leave it ? Sayonara.

Ms. Kim appears to have a personal axe to grind with this country that has given her so much freedom and opportunity.... I should suggest that she move to Korea, where her children will learn all they ever wanted about that country's history.

[Her] whining about the supposedly racist U.S. society is just a mask for her own acute inferiority complex. If she is so dissatisfied with the United States why doesn't she vote with her feet and leave? She can get the hell out and return to her beloved Korea—her tribal afinity [*sic*] where her true loyalty and consciousness lies[*sic*].

You refer to yourself as a Korean American and yet you have lived all your life in the United States.... you write about racism in this country and yet you are the biggest racist by your own written words. If you cannot accept the fact that you are an American, maybe you should be living your life in Korea.

My stepfather and cousin risked their lives in the country where your father is buried to ensure the ideals of our country would remain. So don't expect to find a sympathetic ear for your pathetic whining.

Many of the letter writers assumed that my family had been the "scum" of Asia and that I was a college teacher only because of American justice and largesse[1]. They were furious that I did not express gratitude for being saved from starvation in Asia and given the opportunity to flourish, no doubt beyond my wildest dreams[2], in America.

Where would she be if her parents had not migrated to the United Stated? For a professor at Berkeley University [*sic*] to say the American dram is only an empty promise is ludicrous. Shame, shame, shame on

1. Largesse is a generous gift of money or a generous act of kindness.
2. If you say that you could not imagine a particular thing in your wildest dreams, you are emphasizing that you think it is extremely strange or unlikely. * Never in my wildest dreams did I think we could win.

> Elaine!
>
> [Her father and his family] made enough money in the USA to ship his corpse home to Korea for burial. Ms. Kim herself no doubt has a guaranteed life income as a professor paid by California taxpayers. Wouldn't you think that she might say kind things about the USA instead of whining about racism?

At the same time some letters blamed me for expecting "freedom and opportunity":

> It is wondrous that folks such as you find truth in your paranoia. No one ever promised anything to you or your parents.

Besides providing indications of how Korean Americans are regarded, the letters revealed a great deal about how American identity is thought of. One California woman explained that although her grandparents were Irish immigrants, she was not as Irish American, because "if you are not with us, you are against us." A Missouri woman did not seem to realize that she was conflating race and nationality and confusing "nonethnic" and "nonracial," by which she seems to have meant "white," with "American." And, although she insists that it is impossible to be both "black" and "American," she identifies herself at the outset as a "white American."

> I am a white American. I am proud to be an American. You cannot be black, white, Korean, Chinese, Mexican, German, French, or English or any other and still be an American. Of course the culture taught in schools is strictly American. That's where we are and if you choose to learn another [culture] you have the freedom to settle there. You cannot be a Korean American which assumes you are not ready to be an AMERICAN. Do you get my gist?

The suggestion that more should be taught in U.S. schools about America's many immigrant groups and people of color prompted many letters in defense of Western civilization against non-Western barbarism:

> You are dissatisfied with current school curricula that excludes Korea. Could it possibly be because Korea and Asia for that matter has [sic] not had . . . a noticeable impact on the shaping of Western culture, and Korea has had unfortunately little culture of its own?
>
> Who cares about Korea, Ms. Kim? . . . And what enduring contributions has the Black culture, both here in the US and on the continent contributed to the world, and mankind? I'm from a culture, Ms. Kim, who put a man on the moon 23 years ago, who established medical schools to train doctors to perform open heart surgery, and . . . who created a language of music so that musicians, from Beethoven to the Beatles, could easily touch the world with their brilliance forever and ever and ever. Perhaps the dominant culture, whites obviously, "swept aside Chicanos . . . Latinos . . . African-Americans . . . Koreans," because they haven't contributed anything that made—be mindful of the cliche—a world of difference?
>
> Koreans' favorite means of execution is decapitation . . . Ms. Kim, and others like her, came here to escape such injustice. Then they whine at riots to which they have contributed by their own fanning of flames of discontent . . Yes! Let us all study more about Oriental culture! Let us put matters into proper perspective.
>
> Fanatical multiculturalists like you expect a country whose dominant culture has been formed and influenced by Europe . . . , nearly 80% of her population consisting of persons whose ancestry is European, to include the history of every ethnic group who has ever lived here. I truly feel sorry for you. You and your bunch need to realize that white Americans are not racists. . . . We would love to get along, but not at the expense of our own culture and heritage.
>
> Kim's axe-to-grind confirms the utter futility of race-relations — the races were never meant to live together We don't get along and never will. . . . Whats [sic] needed is to divide the United States up along racial lines so that life here can finally become livable.

What seemed to anger some people the most was their idea that, although they worked hard, people of color were seeking handouts and privileges because of their race, and the thought of an ungrateful Asian American siding with African Americans, presumably against whites, was infuriating. How dare I "bite the hand that feeds" me by siding with the champion "whiners who cry 'racism'" because to do so is the last refuge of the "terminally incompetent"?

> The racial health in this country won't improve until minorities stop erecting "me first" barriers and strive to be Americans, not African-Americans or Asian-Americans expecting privileges.
>
> Ms. Kim wants preferential treatment that immigrants from Greece-to-Sweden have not enjoyed. . . . Even the Chinese . . . have not created any special problems for themselves or other Americans. Soon those folk are going to express their own resentments to the insatiable demands of the Blacks and other colored peoples, including the wetbacks from Mexico who sneak into this country then pilfer it for all they can.
>
> The Afroderived citizens of Los Angeles and the Asiatic derivatives were not suffering a common imposition. . . . The Asiatic are trying to build their success. The Africans are sucking at the teats of entitlement.

As is usual with racists, most of the writers of these hate letters saw only themselves in their notions about Korea, America, Korean Americans, African Americans. They felt that their own sense of American identity was being threatened and that they were being blamed as individuals for U.S. racism. One man, adept at manipulating various fonts on his word processor, imposed his preconceptions on my words:

> Let me read between the lines of your little hate message:
>
> . . . "The roots . . . stretch far back into the corridors of corporate and government offices in Los Angeles, Sacramento, and Washington, D.C."

All white America and all American institutions are to blame for racism.

. . . "I still want to believe the promise is real."

I have the savvy to know that the American ideals of freedom and justice are a joke but if you want to give me what I want I'm willing to make concessions.

Ms. Kim. . . . if you want to embody the ignorant, the insecure, and the emotionally immature, that's your right! Just stop preaching hate and please, please, quit whining.

Sincerely, A proud White-American teaching
my children not to be prejudicial

Especially since my essay had been subdued and intensely personal, I had not anticipated the fury it would provoke. I never thought that readers would write over my words with their own. The very fact that I used words, and English words at that, particularly incensed some: one letter writer complained about my use of words and phrases like "manifestation" and "zero-sum game[1]," and "suzerain relationship," which is the only way to describe Korea's relationship with China during the T'ang Dynasty. "Not more than ten people in the USA know what [these words] mean," he wrote. "You are on an ego trip." I wondered if it made him particularly angry that an Asian American had used those English words, or if he would make such a comment to George Will or Jane Bryant Quinn.

Clearly I had encountered part of America's legacy, the legacy that insists on silencing certain voices and erasing certain presences, even if it means deportation, internment, and outright murder. I should not have been surprised by what happened in Koreatown or by the ignorance and hatred expressed in the letters to *Newsweek*, any more than African Americans should have been

1. If you refer to a situation as a zero-sum game, you mean that if one person gains an advantage from it, someone else involved must suffer an equivalent disadvantage.

surprised by the Rodney King verdict. Perhaps the news media, which constituted *sa-i-ku* as news, as an extraordinary event in no way continuous with our everyday lives, made us forget for a moment that as people of color many of us simultaneously inhabit two Americas: the America of our dreams and the America of our experience.

Who among us does not cling stubbornly to the America of our dreams, the promise of a multicultural democracy where our cultures and our differences might be affirmed instead of distorted in an effort to destroy us?

After sa-i-ku, I was able to catch glimpses of this America of my dreams because I received other litters that expressed another American legacy. Some people identified themselves as Norwegian or Irish Americans interested in combating racism. Significantly, while most of the angry mail had been sent not to me but to *Newsweek*, almost all of the sympathetic mail, particularly the letters from African Americans, came directly to me. Many came from Korean Americans who were glad that one of their number had found a vehicle for self-expression. Others were from Chinese and Japanese Americans who wrote that they had had similar experiences and feelings. Several were written in shaky longhand by women fervently wishing for peace and understanding among people of all races. A Native American from Nashville wrote a long description of cases of racism against African, Asian, and Native Americans in the U.S. criminal-justice system. A large number of letters came from African Americans, all of them supportive and sympathetic — from judges and professors who wanted better understanding between Africans and Koreans to poets and laborers who scribbled their notes in pencil while on breaks at work. One man identified himself as a Los Angeles African American whose uncle had married a Korean woman. He stated that as a black man in America, he knew what other people feel when they face injustice. he ended his letter apologizing for his spelling and grammar mistakes and asking for materials to read on Asian Americans, The most touching letter I received was written by a prison inmate who had served twelve years of a 35-to-70-year sentence for armed robbery during which no physical injures occurred. He wrote:

> I've been locked in these prisons going on 12 years now . . . and since being here I have studied fully the struggles of not just blacks, but all people of color. I am a true believer of helping "your" people "first," but also the helping of all people no matter where there at or the color of there skin. But I must be truthful, my struggle and assistance is truly on the side of people of color like ourselves. But just a few years ago I didn't think like this.
>
> I thought that if you wasn't black, then you was the enemy, but . . . many ars of this prison madness and much study and research changed all of this. . . . [I]t's not with each other, blacks against Koreans or Korean against blacks. No, this is not what it's about.
> Our struggle(s) are truly one in the same. What happened in L.A. during the riot really hurt me, because it was no way that blacks was suppose to do the thing to your people, my people (Koreans) that they did. You're my sister, our people are my people. Even though our culture may be somewhat different, and even though we may worship our God(s) different . . . white-Amerkkka [doesn't] separate us. They look at us all the same. Either you're white, or you're wrong. . . . I'm just writing you to let you know that, you're my sister, your people's struggle are my people's struggle.

This is the ground I need to claim now for Korean American resistance and recovery, so that we can become American without dying of *han*.

Although the sentiments expressed in these letters seemed to break down roughly along racial lines—that is, all writers who were identifiably people of color wrote in support—and one might become alarmed at the depth of the divisions they imply, I like to think that I have experienced the desire of many Americans, especially Americans of color, to do as Rodney King pleaded on the second day of sa-i-ku: "We're all stuck here for awhile. . . . Let's try to work it out."

In my view, it's important for us to think about all of what Rodney King said and not just the words "we all can get along," which have been depoliticized and transformed into a Disneyesque catchphrase for Pat Boone songs and roadside billboards in Los Angeles. It seems to me the emphasis is on the being "stuck here for awhile" together as we await "our day in court."

Like the African American man who wrote from prison, the African American man who had been brutally beaten by white police might have felt the desire to "love everybody," but he had to amend—or rectify—that wish. He had to speak last about loving "people of color." The impulse to "love everybody" was there, but the conditions were not right. For now, the most practical and progressive agenda may be people of color trying to "work it out."

FINDING COMMUNITY THROUGH NATIONAL CONSCIOUSNESS

The place where Korean and American legacies converge for Korean Americans is the exhortation to "go home to where you belong."

One of the letters I received was from a Korean American living in Chicago. He had read a translation of my essay in a Korean language newspaper. "Although you were born in the U.S.A," he wrote, noticing what none of the white men who ordered me to go back to "my" country had, "your ethnical background and your complexion belong to Korea. It is time to give up your U.S. citizenship and go to Korea."

Some ruined merchants are claiming that they will pull up stakes and return to Korea, but I know that this is not possible for most of them. Even if their stores had not been destroyed, even if they were able to sell their businesses and take the proceeds to Korea, most of them would not have enough to buy a home or business there, since both require total cash up front. Neither would they be able to find work in the society they left behind because it is plagued by recession, repression, and fierce economic competition.

Going back to Korea. The dream of going back Korea fed the spirit of my father, who came to Chicago in 1926 and lived in the United States for 63 years, during which time he never became a U.S. citizen, at first because the law did not allow it and later because he did not want to. He kept himself going by believing that he would return to Korea in triumph one day. Instead, he died in Oakland at 88. Only his remains returned to Korea, where we buried him in accordance with his wishes.

Hasn't the dream of going back home to where you belong sustained most of America's unwanted at one time or another, giving meaning to lives of toil and making it possible to endure other people's hatred and rejection? Isn't the attempt to find community through national consciousness natural for people refused an American identity because racism does not give them that choice?

Korean national consciousness, the resolve to resist and fight back when threatened with extermination, was all that could be called upon when the Korean Americans in Los Angeles found themselves abandoned. They joined together to guard each other's means of livelihood with guns, relying on Korean-language radio and newspapers to communicate with and help each other. On the third day after the outbreak of violence, more than 30,000 Korean Americans gathered for a peace march in downtown L.A. in what was perhaps the largest and most quickly organized mass mobilization in Asian American history. Musicians in white, the color of mourning, beat traditional Korean drums in sorrow, anger, and celebration of community a call to arms like a collective heartbeat. I believe that the mother of Edward Song Lee, the Los Angeles-born college student mistaken for a looter and shot to death in the streets, has been able to persevere in great part because of the massive outpouring of sympathy expressed by the Korean-American community that shared and understood her *han*.

I have been critical lately of cultural nationalism as detrimental to Korean Americans, especially Korean American women, because it operates on exclusions and fosters intolerance and uniformity of thought while stifling self-criticism and encouraging sacrifice, even to the point of suicide. But *sa-i-ku* makes me think again: what remains for those who are left to stand alone? If Korean Americans refuse to be victims or political pawns in the U.S. while rejecting the exhortation that we go back to Korea where we belong, what will be our weapons of choice?

In the darkest days of Japanese colonial rule, even after being stripped of land and of all economic means of survival, Koreans were threatened with total erasure when the colonizers rewrote Korean history, outlawed the Korean language, forced the subjugated people to worship the Japanese emperor, and demanded that they adopt Japanese names. One of the results of these cultural-annihilation policies was Korean's fierce insistence on the sanctity[1] of Korean national identity that persists to this day. In this context, it is not difficult to understand why nationalism has been the main refuge of Korean and Korean Americans.

While recognizing the potential dangers of nationalism as a weapon, I for one am not ready to respond to the antiessentialists' call to relinquish my Koran American identity. It is easy enough for the French and Germans to call for a common Europen identity and an end to nationalisms, but what of the peoples suppressed and submerged while France and Germany exercise their national prerogatives? I am mindful of[2] the argument that the resurgence of nationalism in Europe is rooted in historical and contemporary political and economic inequality among the nations of Europe. Likewise, I have noticed that many white Americans do not like to think of themselves as belonging to a race, even while thinking of people of color almost exclusively in terms of race. In the same way, many men think of themselves as "human beings" and of women as the ones having a gender. Thus crime, small businesses, and all Korean-African American interactions are seen and interpreted through the lens of race in the same dominant culture that angrily rejects the use of the racial lens for viewing yellow/white or black/white interactions and insists suddenly that we are all "American" whenever we attempt to assert our identity as people of color. It is far easier for Anglo Americans to call for an end to cultural nationalisms than for Korean Americans to give up national consciousness, which makes it possible to survive the vicious racism that would deny our existence as either Korean Americans or Americans.

Is there anything of use to us in Korean nationalism? During one thousand years of Chinese suzerainty, the Korean ruling elite developed a philosophy called *sadaejui*, or reliance of the

1. If you talk about the sanctity of something, you mean that it is very important and must be treated with respect.
2. If you are mindful of something, you think about it and consider it when taking action. (=aware)

weak on the strong. In direct opposition to this way of thought is what is called jaju or juche sasang, or self-determination. Both *sadaejui* and *juche sasang* are ways of dealing with unequal power relationships and resisting the transformation of one's homeland into a battlefield for others, but sadaejui has never worked any better for Koreans than it has for any minority group in America. Juche sasang, on the other hand, has the kind of oppositional potential needed in the struggle against silence and invisibility. From Korean national consciousness, we can recover this fierce refusal to accept subjugation, which is the first step in the effort to build community, so that we can work with others to challenge the forces that would have us annihilate each other instead of our mutual oppression.

What is clear is that we cannot "become American" without dying of *han* unless we think about community in new ways. Self-determination does not mean living alone. At least for now, that may mean mining the rich and haunted lode of Korean national consciousness while we struggle to understand how our rate is entwined with the fate of others lying prostrate before the triumphal procession of the winners of History. During the past fifteen years or so, many young Korean nationalists have been studying the legacies of colonialism and imperialism that they share with peoples in many Asian, African, and Latin American nations. At the same time that we take note of this work, we can also try to understand how nationalism and feminism can be worked together to demystify the limitations and reductiveness of each as a weapon of empowerment. If Koran national consciousness is ever to be such a weapon for us, we must use it to create a new kind of nationalism-in-internationalism to help us call forth a culture of survival and recovery, so that our *han* might be released and we might be freed to dream fiercely of different possibilities.

AFTER YOU READ

1. What does the writer think of Los Angeles Koreatown?

2. Who had redifined the meaning of Americans in 1960s?

3. Why could the writer hardly believe her ears during the weeks immediately following *sa-i-ku*?

4. When she overheard European Americans discussing the conflicts as if they were watching a dogfight or boxing match, what did the situation remind her of?

5. Did most Korean immigrants know they were among the many direct beneficiaries of the African American-led civil rights movement?

6. Who were desperate to believe that the American dream of social and economic mobility through hard work was within their reach?

7. What makes it possible to survive the vicious racism that would deny their existence as either Korean Americans or Americans?

15

MARGARET THATCHER: THE LADY'S NOT FOR TURNING SPEECH TO CONSERVATIVE PARTY CONFERENCE DELIVERED ON 10 OCTOBER, 1980

by Margaret Thatcher

Mr. chairman, ladies and gentlemen, most of my Cabinet colleagues have started their speeches of reply by paying very well deserved tributes to their junior Ministers. At Number 10 I have no junior Ministers. There is just [Denis Thatcher] Denis and me, and I could not do without him.

I am, however, very fortunate in having a marvellous deputy who is wonderful in all places at all times in all things—Willie Whitelaw.

At our party conference last year I said that the task in which the Government were engaged—to change the national attitude of mind—was the most challenging to face any British Administration since the war. Challenge is exhilarating. This week we Conservatives have been taking stock[1], discussing the achievements, the set-backs[2] and the work that lies ahead as we enter our second parliamentary year. As you said Mr Chairman our debates have been stimulating and our debates have been constructive. This week has demonstrated that we are a party united in purpose, strategy and resolve. And we actually like one another.

---

1. If you take stock, you pause to think about all the aspects of a situation or event before deciding what to do next.
   * It was time to take stock of the situation.
2. A setback is an event that delays your progress or reserve some of the progress that you have made.

When I am asked for a derailed forecast of what will happen in the coming months or years I remember Sam Goldwyn's advice: "Never prophesy, especially about the future." (Interruption from the floor) Never mind, it is wet outside. I expect that they wanted to come in. You cannot blame them; it is always better where the Tories are. And you—and perhaps they—will be looking to me this afternoon for an indication of how the Government see the task before us and why we are tackling it the way we are. Before I begin let me get one thing out of the way.

This week at Brighton we have heard a good deal about last week at Blackpool. I will have a little more to say about that strange assembly later, but for the moment I want to say just this.

Because of what happened at that conference, there has been, behind all our deliberations[1] this week, a heightened awareness that now, more than ever, our Conservative Government must succeed. We just must, because now there is even more at stake than some had realised.

There are many things to be done to set this nation on the road to recovery, and I do not mean economic recovery alone, but a new independence of spirit and zest for achievement.

It is sometimes said that because of our past we, as a people, expect too much and set our sights too high. That is not the way I see it. Rather it seems to me that throughout my life in politics our ambitions have steadily shrunk. Our response to disappointment has not been to lengthen our stride but to shorten the distance to be covered. But with confidence in ourselves and in our future what a nation we could be!

In its first seventeen months this Government have laid the foundations for recovery. We have undertaken a heavy load of legislation, a load we do not intend to repeat because we do not share the Socialist fantasy that achievement is measured by the number of laws you pass. But there was a formidable barricade

---

1. Deliberations is the long and careful consideration of a subject.

of obstacles that we had to sweep aside. For a start, in his first Budget Geoffrey Howe began to rest incentives to stimulate the abilities and inventive genius of our people. Prosperity comes not from grand conferences of economists but by countless acts of personal self-confidence and self-reliance.

Under Geoffrey's stewardship, Britain has repaid $3,600 million of international debt, debt which had been run up[1] by our predecessors. And we paid quite a lot of it before it was due. In the past twelve months Geoffrey has abolished exchange controls over which British Governments have dithered[2] for decades. Our great enterprises are now free to seek opportunities overseas. This will help to secure our living standards long after North Sea oil has run out. This Government thinks about the future. We have made the first crucial changes in trade union law to remove the worst abuses of the closed shop, to restrict picketing to the place of work of the parties in dispute, and to encourage secret ballots.

Jim Prior has carried all these measures through with the support of the vast majority of trade union members. Keith Joseph, David Howell, John Nott and Norman Fowler have began to break down the monopoly powers of nationalisation. Thanks to them British Aerospace will soon be open to private investment. The monopoly of the post Office and British Telecommunications is being diminished. The barriers to private generation of electricity for sale have been lifted. For the first time nationalised industries and public utilities can be investigated by the Monopolies Commission—a long overdue[3] reform.

Free competition in road passenger transport promises travellers a better deal. Michael Heseltine has given to millions—yes, millions—of council tenants the right to buy their own homes.

1. If someone runs up bills or debts, they acquire them by buying a lot of things or borrowing money.(외상이나 빚을 지다)
2. When someone dithers, they hesitate because they are unable to make a quick decision about something
3. If you say that a change or an event is overdue, you mean that you think it should have happened before now

It was Anthony Eden who chose for us the goal of "a property-owning democracy". But for all the time that I have been in public affairs that has been beyond the reach of so many, who were denied the right to the most basic ownership of all—the homes in which they live.

They wanted to buy. Many could afford to buy. But they happened to live under the jurisdiction of a Socialist council, which would not sell and did not believe in the independence that comes with ownership. Now Michael Heseltine has given them the chance to turn a dream into reality, And all this and a lot more in seventeen months.

The Left continues to refer with relish to the death of capitalism. Well, if this is the death of capitalism, I must say that it is quite a way to go.

But all this will avail us little unless we achieve our prime economic objective—the defeat of inflation. Inflation destroys nations and societies as surely as invading armies do. Inflation is the parent of unemployment. It is the unseen robber of those who have saved.

No policy which puts at risk the defeat of inflation—however great its short-term attraction—can be right. Our policy for the defeat of inflation is, in fact, traditional. It existed long before Sterling M3 embellished the Bank of England Quarterly Bulletin, or "monetarism" became a convenient term of political invective[1].

But some people talk as if control of the money supply was a revolutionary policy. Yet it was an essential condition for the recovery of much of continental Europe.

Those countries knew what was required for economic stability. Previously, they had lived through rampant inflation; they knew that it led to suitcase money, massive unemployment

1. Invective is rude and unpleasant things that people shout at people they hate or are angry with.

and the breakdown of society itself. They determined never to go that way again.

Today, after many years of monetary self-discipline, they have stable, prosperous economies better able than ours to withstand the buffeting[1] of world recession.

So at international conferences to discuss economic affairs many of my fellow Heads of Government find our policies not strange, unusual or revolutionary, but normal, sound and honest. And that is what they are.

Their only question is: "Has Britain the courage and resolve to sustain the discipline for long enough to break through to success?"

Yes Mr. Chairman, we have, and we shall. This Government are determined to stay with the policy and see it through to its conclusion. That is what marks this administration as one of the truly radical ministries of post-war Britain. Inflation is falling and should continue to fall.

Meanwhile we are not heedless of the hardships and worries that accompany the conquest of inflation.

Foremost among these is unemployment. Today our country has more than 2 million unemployed.

Now you can try to soften that figure in a dozen ways. You can point out—and it is quite legitimate to do so — that 2 million today does not mean what it meant in the 1930s; that the percentage of unemployment is much less now than it was then.

You can add that today many more married women go out to work.

1. If an economy or government is buffeted by difficult or unpleasant situations, it experiences many of them.

You can stress that, because of the high birthrate in the early 1960s, there is an unusually large number of school leavers this year looking for work and that the same will be true for the next two years.

You can emphasise that about a quarter of a million people find new jobs each month and therefore go off the employment register.

And you can recall that there are nearly 25 million people in jobs compared with only about 18 million in the 1930s. You can point out that the Labour party conveniently overlooks the fact that of the 2 million unemployed for which they blame us, nearly a million and a half were bequeathed by their Government.

But when all that has been said the fact remains that the level of unemployment in our country today is a human tragedy. Let me make it clear beyond doubt. I am profoundly concerned about unemployment. Human dignity and self respect are undermined when men and women are condemned to idleness. The waste of a country's most precious assets — the talent and energy of its people—makes it the bounden[1] duty of Government to seek a real and lasting cure.

If I could press a button and genuinely solve the unemployment problem, do you think that I would not press that button this instant? Does anyone imagine that there is the smallest political gain in letting this unemployment continue, or that there is some obscure economic religion which demands this unemployment as part of its ritual? This Government are pursuing the only policy which gives any hope of bringing our people back to real and lasting employment. It is no coincidence that those countries, of which I spoke earlier, which have had lower rates of inflation have also had lower levels of unemployment.

I know that there is another real worry affecting many of our

---

1. bounden : obligatory, compulsory

people. Although they accept that our policies are right, they feel deeply that the burden of carrying them out is falling much more heavily on the private than on the public sector. They say that the public sector is enjoying advantages but the private sector is taking the knocks and at the same time maintaining those in the public sector with better pay and pensions than they enjoy.

I must tell you that I share this concern and understand the resentment. That is why I and my colleagues say that to add to public spending takes away the very money and resources that industry needs to stay in business let alone to expand. Higher public spending, far from curing unemployment, can be the very vehicle that loses jobs and causes bankruptcies in trade and commerce. That is why we warned local authorities that since rates are frequently the biggest tax that industry now faces, increases in them can cripple local businesses. Councils must, therefore, learn to cut costs in the same way that companies have to.

That is why I stress that if those who work in public authorities take for themselves large pay increases they leave less to be spent on equipment and new buildings. That in turn deprives the private sector of the orders it needs, especially some of those industries in the hard pressed regions. Those in the public sector have a duty to those in the private sector not to take out so much in pay that they cause others unemployment. That is why we point out that every time high wage settlements in nationalised monopolies lead to higher charges for telephones, electricity, coal and water, they can drive companies out of business and cost other people their jobs.

If spending money like water was the answer to our country's problems, we would have no problems now. If ever a nation has spent, spent, spent and spent again, ours has. Today that dream is over. All of that money has got us nowhere but it still has to come from somewhere. Those who urge us to relax the squeeze, to spend yet more money indiscriminately in the belief that it will help the unemployed and the small businessman are not being kind or compassionate or caring.

They are not the friends of the unemployed or the small business. They are asking us to do again the very thing that caused the problems in the first place. We have made this point repeatedly.

I am accused of lecturing or preaching about this. I suppose it is a critic's way of saying "Well, we know it is true, but we have to carp[1] at something." I do not care about that. But I do care about the future of free enterprise, the jobs and exports it provides and the independence it brings to our people. Independence? Yes, but let us be clear what we mean by that. Independence does not mean contracting out of all relationships with others. A nation can be free but it will not stay free for long if it has no friends and no alliances. Above all, it will not stay free if it cannot pay its own way in the world. By the same token[2], an individual needs to be part of a community and to feel that he is part of it. There is more to this than the chance to earn a living for himself and his family, essential though that is.

Of course, our vision and our aims go far beyond the complex arguments of economics, but unless we get the economy right we shall deny our people the opportunity to share that vision and to see beyond the narrow horizons of economic necessity. Without a healthy economy we cannot have a healthy society. Without a healthy society the economy will not stay healthy for long.

But it is not the State that creates a healthy society. When the State grows too powerful people feel that they count for less and less. The State drains society, not only of its wealth but of initiative, of energy, the will to improve and innovate as well as to preserve what is best. Our aim is to let people feel that they count for more and more. If we cannot trust the deepest instincts of our people we should not be in politics at all. Some aspect of our present society really do offend those instincts.

Decent people do want to do a proper job at work, not to be restrained or intimidated from giving value for money. They

1. If you say that someone is carping, you mean that they keep criticizing or complaining about someone or something, especially in a way you think is unnecessary or annoying.
2. by the same token : moreover, furthermore

believe that honesty should be respected, not derided. They see crime and violence as a threat not just to society but to their own orderly way of life. They want to be allowed to bring up their children in these beliefs, without the fear that their efforts will be daily frustrated in the name of progress or free expression. Indeed, that is what family life is all about.

There is not a generation gap in a happy and united family. People yearn to be able to rely on some generally accepted standards. Without them you have not got a society at all, you have purposeless anarchy. A healthy society is not created by its institutions, either. Great schools and universities do not make a great nation any more than great armies do. Only a great nation can create and involve great institutions — of learning, of healing, of scientific advance. And a great nation is the voluntary creation of its people — a people composed of men and women whose pride in themselves is founded on the knowledge of what they can give to a community of which they in turn can be proud.

If our people feel that they are part of a great nation and they are prepared to will the means to keep it great, a great nation we shall be, and shall remain. So, what can stop us from achieving this? What then stands in our way? The prospect of another winter of discontent? I suppose it might.

But I prefer to believe that certain lessons have been learnt from experience, that we are coming, slowly, painfully, to an autumn of understanding. And I hope that it will be followed by a winter of common sense. If it is not, we shall not be — diverted from our course.

To those waiting with bated breath[1] for that favourite media catchphrase, the "U" turn, I have only one thing to say. "You turn if you want to. The lady's not for turning." I say that not only to you but to our friends overseas and also to those who are not our

1. If you wait for something with bated breath, you wait anxiously to find out what will happen.

friends.

In foreign affairs we have pursued our national interest robustly while remaining alive to the needs and interests of others. We have acted where our predecessors dithered and here I pay tribute to Lord Carrington. When I think of our much-travelled Foreign Secretary I am reminded of the advert, you know the one I mean, about "The peer that reaches those foreign parts that other peers cannot reach."

Long before we came into office, and therefore long before the invasion of Afghanistan I was pointing to the threat from the East. I was accused of scaremongering[1]. But events have more than justified my words.

Soviet Marxism is ideologically, politically and morally bankrupt. But militarily the Soviet Union is a powerful and growing threat.

Yet it was Mr. Kosygin who said "No peace loving country, no person of integrity, should remain indifferent when an aggressor holds human life and world opinion in insolent contempt." We agree. The British Government are not indifferent to the occupation[2] of Afghanistan. We shall not allow it to be forgotten. Unless and until the Soviet troops are withdrawn other nations are bound to wonder which of them may be next. Of course there are those who say that by speaking out we are complicating East-West relations, that we are endangering detente. But the real danger would lie in keeping silent. Detente is indivisible and it is a two-way process.

The Soviet Union cannot conduct wars by proxy in South-East Asia and Africa, foment trouble in Middle East and Caribbean and invade neighbouring countries and still expect to conduct

---

1. If one person or group accuses anther person or group of scaremongering, they accuse them of deliberately spreading worrying stories to try and frighten people.
2. The occupation of a country happens when it is entered and controlled by a foreign army.

business as usual. Unless detente is pursued by both sides it can be pursued by neither, and it is a delusion to suppose otherwise. That is the message we shall be delivering loud and clear at the meeting of the European Security Conference in Madrid in the weeks immediately ahead.

But we shall also be reminding the other parties in Madrid that the Helsinki Accord was supposed to promote the freer movement of people and ideas. The Soviet Government's response so far has been a campaign of repression worse than any since Stalin's day. It had been hoped that Helsinki would open gates across Europe. In fact the guards today are better armed and the walls are no lower. But behind those walls the human spirit is unvanquished.

The workers of Poland in their millions have signalled their determination to participate in the shaping of their destiny. We salute them.

Marxists claim that the capitalist system is in crisis. But the Polish workers have shown that it is the Communist system that is in crisis. The Polish people should be left to work out their own future without external interference.

At every party Conference, and every November in parliament, we used to face difficult decisions over Rhodesia and over sanctions. But no longer. Since we last met the success at Lancaster house, and thereafter in Salisbury—a success won in the face of all the odds—has created new respect for Britain. It has given fresh hope to those grappling with the terrible problems of Southern Africa. It has given the Commonwealth new strength and unity. Now it is for the new nation, Zimbabwe, to build her own future with the support of all those who believe that democracy has a place in Africa, and we wish her well.

We showed over Rhodesia that hallmarks of Tory policy are, as they have always been, realism and resolve. Not for us the disastrous fantasies of unilateral disarmament, of withdrawal from NATO, of abandoning Northern ireland.

The irresponsibility of the Left on defence increases as the dangers which we face loom larger. We for our part, under Francis Pym's brilliant leadership, have chosen a defence policy which potential foes will respect.

We are acquiring, with the co-operation of the United States Government, the Trident missile system. This will ensure the credibility of our strategic deterrent until the end of the century and beyond, and it was very important for the reputation of Britain abroad, and that we should keep our independent nuclear deterrent as well as for our citizens here.

We have agreed to the stationing of Cruise missiles in this country. The unilateralists object, but the recent willingness of the Soviet Government to open a new round of arms control negotiations shows the wisdom of our firmness.

We intend to maintain and, where possible, to improve our conventional forces so as to pull our weight in the Alliance. We have no wish to seek a free ride at the expense of our Allies. We will play our full part.

In Europe we have shown that it is possible to combine a vigorous defence of our own interests with a deep commitment to the idea and to the ideals of the Community.

The last Government were well aware that Britain's budget contribution was grossly[1] unfair. They failed to do anything about it. We negotiated a satisfactory arrangement which will give us and our partners time to tackle the underlying issues. We have resolved the difficulties of New Zealand's lamb trade with the Community in a way which protects the interests of the farmers in New Zealand while giving our own farmers and our own housewives an excellent deal, and Peter Walker deserves to be congratulated on his success. Now he is two-thirds on his way to success in making important progress towards agreement on

1. grossly : completely

a common fisheries policy. That is very important to our people. There are many, many people whose livelihoods depend on it.

We face many other problems in the Community, but I am confident that they too will yield to the firm yet fair approach which has already proved so much more effective than the previous Government's five years of procrastination.

With each day it becomes clearer that in the wider world we face darkening horizons, and the war between Iran and Iraq is the latest symptom of a deeper malady. Europe and North America are centres of stability in an increasingly anxious world. The Community and the Alliance are the guarantee to other countries that democracy and freedom of choice are still possible. They stand for order and the rule of law in an age when disorder and lawlessness are ever more widespread.

The British Government intend to stand by both these great institutions, the Community and NATO. We will not betray them.

The restoration of Britain's place in the world and of the West's confidence in its own destiny are two aspects of the same process. No doubt there will be unexpected twists in the road, but with wisdom and resolution we can reach our goal. I believe we will show the wisdom and you may be certain that we will show the resolution.

In his warm hearted and generous speech, Peter Thorneycroft said that, when people are called upon to lead great nations they must look into the hearts and minds of the people whom they seek to govern. I would add that those who seek to govern must in turn be willing to allow their hearts and minds to lie open to the people.

This afternoon I have tried to set before you some of my most deeply held convictions and beliefs. This Party, which I am privileged to serve, and this Government, which I am proud to lead, are engaged in the massive task of restoring confidence and stability to our people.

I have always known that that task was vital. Since last week it has become even more vital than ever. We close our Conference in the aftermath of that sinister Utopia unveiled at Blackpool. Let Labour's Orwellian nightmare of the Left be the spur for us to dedicate with a new urgency our every ounce of energy and moral strength to rebuild the fortunes of this free nation.

If we were to fail, that freedom could be imperilled. So let us resist the blandishments[1] of the faint hearts; let us ignore the howls and threats of the extremists; let us stand together and do our duty, and we shall not fail.

1. Blandishments are pleasant things that someone says to another person in order to persuade them to do something. (=flattery)

After You Read

1. Mrs. Thatcher said, "There are many things to be done to set this nation on the road to recovery." What are they?

2. According to her, what is their prime economic objective?

3. What did she think was an essential condition for the recovery of much of continental Europe?

4. Foremost among the hardships and worries that accompany the conquest of inflation is.______________________________.

5. She said, "There is more to this than the chance to earn a living for himself and his family. What is this?

6. What does she define a great nation?

7. According to her, what must those who seek to govern do?

16

WINSTON CHURCHILL:

THE SINEWS[1] OF PEACE
DELIVERED ON MARCH 5, 1946

by Winston Churchill

President McCluer, ladies and gentleman, and last but certainly not least, President of the United States of America:

I am very glad indeed to come to Westminster College this afternoon, and I am complimented that you should give me a degree from an institution whose reputation has been so solidly established. The name "Westminster" somehow or other seems familiar to me. I—I feel as if I've heard of it before. Indeed now that I come to think of it, it was at Westminster that I received a very large part of my education in politics, dialectic, rhetoric—and one or two other things. So, in fact we have both been educated at the same, or similar, or, at any rate, kindred[2] establishments.

It is also an honor, ladies and gentleman, perhaps almost unique, for a private visitor to be introduced to an academic audience by the President of the United States. Amid his heavy burdens, duties, and responsibilities—unsought but not recoiled from—the President has traveled a thousand miles to dignify and magnify our meeting here today and to give me an opportunity of addressing this kindred nation, as well as my own countrymen across the ocean, and—and perhaps some other countries too.

---

1. A sinew is a cord in your body that connects a muscle to a bone.
2. Kindrid things are similar to each other.
   *I recall many discussions with her on these and kindred topics.

The—The President has told you that it is his wish, as I am sure it is yours, that I should have full liberty to give my true and faithful counsel in these anxious and baffling times. Now, I shall certainly avail myself of[1] this freedom, and feel the more right to do so because any private ambitions I may have cherished in my younger days have been satisfied beyond my wildest dreams. Let me, however, make it clear that I have no official mission or status of any kind, and that I speak only for myself. There is nothing here but what you see.

I can therefore allow my mind, with the experience of a lifetime, to play over the problems which beset us on the morrow of our absolute victory in arms, and to try to make sure with what strength I have that what has been gained with so much sacrifice and suffering shall be preserved for the future glory and safety of mankind.

Ladies and gentlemen, the United States stands at this time at the pinnacle of world power. It is a solemn moment for the American democracy. For with primacy in power is also joined an awe-inspiring [2]accountability to the future. If, as you look around you—If you look around you, you must feel not only the sense of duty done but also you must feel anxiety lest you fall below the level of achievement. Opportunity is here now, clear and shining for both our countries. To reject it or ignore it or fritter it away[3] will bring upon us all the long reproaches of the after-time. It is necessary that constancy of mind, persistency of purpose, and the grand simplicity of decision shall rule and guide the conduct of the English-speaking peoples in peace as they did in war. And we must, and I believe we shall, prove ourselves equal

---

1. If you avail yourself of an offer or an opportunity, you accept the offer or make use of the opportunity.
   * Guests should feel at liberty to avail themselves of your facilities.
2. If you describe someone or something as awe-inspring, you are emphasizing that you think that they are remarkable and amazing, although sometimes rather frightening. * The higher we climbed, the more awe-inspring the scenery became.
3. If someone fritters away time or money, they waste it on unimportant or unnecessary things. (=squander)

to this severe requirement.

President McCluer, when American military men approach some serious situation they are wont to[1] write at the head of their directive the words "over-all strategic concept." There is wisdom in this, as it leads to clarity of thought. What then is the overall strategic concept which we should inscribe today? It is nothing less than the safety and welfare, the freedom and progress, of all the homes and families of all the men and women in all the lands. And here I speak particularly of the myriad cottage or apartment homes where the wage-earner strives amid the accidents and difficulties of life to guard his wife and children from privation[2] and bring the family up in the fear of the lord, or upon ethical conceptions which often play their potent part.

To give security to these countless homes, they must be shielded from the two gaunt marauders, war and tyranny. We all know the frightful disturbance in which the ordinary family is plunged when the curse of war swoops down upon the bread-winner and those for whom he works and contrives. The awful ruin of Europe, with all its vanished glories, and of large parts of Asia glares us in the eyes. When the designs of wicked men or the aggressive urge of mighty States dissolve over large areas the frame of civilized society, humble folk are confronted with difficulties with which they cannot cope. For them is all distorted, all is broken, all is even ground to pulp[3].

When I stand here this quiet afternoon I shudder to visualize what is actually happening to millions now and what is going to happen in this period when famine stalks[4] the earth. None can compute what has been called "the unestimated sum of human

1. If someone is wont to do something, they often or regularly do it. (=inclined)

2. If you suffer privation or privations, you have to live without many of the things that are thought to be necessary in life, such as food, clothing, or comfort. * They endured five years of privation during the second world war.
3. be ground to pulp: 펄프 같이 흐믈흐믈 해지다
4. stalk: 만연하다

pain." Our supreme task and duty is to guard the homes of the common people from the horrors and miseries of another war.

We are all agreed on that.

Our American military colleagues, after having proclaimed their "over-all strategic concept" and computed available resources, always proceed to the next step—namely, the method. Here again there is widespread agreement. A world organization has already been erected for the prime purpose of preventing war. UNO—"U-N-O"—the successor of the League of Nations, with the decisive addition of the United States and all that that means, is already at work. We must make sure that its work is fruitful, that it is a reality and not a sham, that it is a force for action, and not merely a frothing[1] of words, that it is a true temple of peace in which the shields of many nations can some day be hung up, and not merely a cockpit in a Tower of Babel. Before we cast away the solid assurances of national armaments for self-preservation we must be certain that our temple is built, not upon shifting sands or quagmires[2], but upon the rock. Anyone can see with his—with his eyes open that our path will be difficult and also long, but if we persevere together as we did in the two world wars—though not, alas[3], in the interval between them—I cannot doubt that we shall achieve our common purpose in the end.

I have, however, a definite and practical proposal to make for action.

Courts and magistrates may be set up but they cannot function without sheriffs and constables. The United Nations Organization must immediately begin to be equipped with an international armed force. In such a matter we can only go step by step, but we must begin now. I propose that each of the Powers and States should be invited to dedicate a certain number

1. frothing: (말의) 거품, 공허함
2. A quagmire is a soft, wet area of land which your feet sink into if you try to walk across it. * Rain had turned the grass into a quagmire.
3. You use alas to say that you think that the facts you are talking about are sad or unfortunate. (=sadly)

of air squadrons[1] to the service of the world organization. These squadrons would be trained and prepared in their own countries, but would move around in rotation from one country to another. They would wear the uniforms of their own countries but with different badges. They would not be required to act against their own nation, but in other respects they would be directed by the world organization. This might be started on a modest scale and it would grow as confidence grew. I wished to see this done after the first world war, and I devoutly trust that it may be done forthwith[2].

It would nevertheless, ladies and gentlemen, be wrong and imprudent to entrust the secret knowledge or experience of the atomic bomb, which the United States, great Britain, and Canada now share, to the world organization, while it is still in its infancy. It would be criminal madness to cast it adrift in this still agitated and un-united world. No one in any country—No one in any country has slept less well in their beds because this knowledge and the method and the raw materials to apply it, are at present largely retained in American hands. I do not believe we should all have slept so soundly had the positions been reversed and some Communist or neo-Fascist State monopolized for the time being these dread agencies. The fear of them alone might easily have been used to enforce totalitarian systems upon the free democratic world, with consequences appalling to human imagination. God has willed that this shall not be and we have at least a breathing space to set our house in order before this peril has to be encountered. And even then, if no effort is spared, we should still possess so formidable a superiority as to impose effective deterrents[3] upon its employment, or threat of employment, by others. Ultimately, when the essential brotherhood of man is truly embodied and expressed in a world organization with all the necessary practical safeguards to make it effective, these powers would naturally be confided to that world organization.

Now I come to the second of the two marauders, to the

1. A squadron is a section of one of the armed forces, especially the air force.
2. Forthwith means immediately.
3. A deterrent is something that prevents people from doing something by making them afraid of what will happen to them if they do it.

second danger which threatens the cottage homes, and ordinary people— namely, tyranny.

We cannot be blind to the fact that the liberties enjoyed by individual citizens throughout the United States and throughout the British Empire are not valid in a considerable number of countries, some of which are very powerful. With these States control is enforced upon the common people by various kinds of all-embracing[1] police governments to a degree which is overwhelming and contray to every principle of democracy. The power of the State is exercised without restraint, either by dictators or by compact oligarchies[2] operating through a privileged party and a political police. It is not our duty at this time when difficulties are so numerous to interfere forcibly in the internal affairs of countries which we have not conquered in war. But we must never cease to proclaim in fearless tones the great principles of freedom and the rights of man which are the joint inheritance of the English-speaking world and which through Magna Carta, the Bill of Rights, the Habeas Corpus, trial by jury, the English common law find their most famous expression in the American Declaration of Independence.

All this means that the people of any country have the right, and should have the power by constitutional action, by free unfettered elections, with secret ballot, to choose or change the character or form of government under which they dwell; that freedom of speech and thought should reign; that courts of justice, independent of the executive, unbiased by any party, should administer laws which have received the broad assent of large majorities or are consecrated by time and custom. Here are the title deeds of freedom which should lie in every cottage home. Here is the message of the British and American peoples to mankind. Let us preach what we practice—let us practice what we preach.

---

1. Something that is all-embracing includes or affects everyone or everything.
   • His hospitality was instantaneous and all-embracing (=all-emcompassing)
2. An oligarchy is a small group of people who control and run a particular country or organization. You can also refer to a country which is governed in this way as an oligarchy.

Though I have now stated the two great dangers which menace the homes of the people, war and tyranny, I have not yet spoken of poverty and privation which are in many cases the prevailing anxiety. But if the dangers of war and tyranny are removed, there is no doubt that science and cooperation can bring in the next few years, certainly in the next few decades, to the world, newly taught in the sharpening school of war, an expansion of material well-being beyond anything that has yet occurred in human experience.

Now, at this sad and breathless moment, we are plunged in the hunger and distress which are the aftermath of our stupendous[1] struggle; but this will pass and may pass quickly, and there is no reason except human folly or sub-human[2] crime which should deny to all the nations the inauguration and enjoyment of an age of plenty. I have often used words which I learned 50 years ago from a great Irish-American orator, a friend of mine, Mr. Bourke Cockran, "There is enough for all. The earth is a generous mother; she will provide in plentiful abundance food for all her children if they will but cultivate her soil in justice and in peace."

And so—So far I—I—I feel that we are in—in full agreement.

Now, while still pursuing the method—the method of realizing our overall strategic concept, I come to the crux of what I have traveled here to say. Neither the sure prevention of war, nor the continuous rise of world organization will be gained without what I have called the fraternal association of the English-speaking peoples. This means a special relationship between the British Commonwealth and Empire and the United States of America. Ladies and gentlemen, this is no time for generalities[3],

1. Something that is stupendous is surprisingly impressive or large.
2. If you describe someone or their situation as subhuman, you mean that they behave or live in a much worse way than human beings normally do. * Greek treated women as subhuman.
3. A generality is a general statement that covers a range of things, rather than being concerned with specific instances. * I'll start with some generalities and then examine a few specific examples.

and I will venture to be precise. Fraternal association requires not only the growing friendship and mutual understanding between our two vast but kindred systems of society, but the continuance of the intimate relations between our military advisers, leading to common study of potential dangers, the similarity of weapons and manuals of instruction, and to the interchange of officers and cadets at technical colleges. It should carry with it the continuance of the present facilities for mutual security by the joint use of all Naval and Air Force bases in the possession of either country all over the world. And this—this would perhaps double the mobility of the American Navy and Air Force. It would greatly expand that of the British Empire forces and it might well lead, if and as the world calms down, to important financial savings. Already we use together a large number of islands; more may well be entrusted to our joint care in the near future.

The United States has already a Permanent Defense Agreement with the Dominion of Canada, which is so devotedly attached to the British Commonwealth and Empire. This Agreement is more effective than many of those which have often been made under formal alliances. This principle should be extended to all the British Commonwealths with full reciprocity[1]. Thus, whatever happens, and thus only, shall we be secure ourselves and able to work together for the high and simple causes that are dear to us and bode[2] no ill to any. Eventually—Eventually there may come—I feel eventually there will come—the principle of common citizenship, but that we may be content to leave to destiny, whose outstretched arm many of us can already clearly see.

There is however an important question we must ask ourselves. Would a—a special relationship between the United States and the British Commonwealth be inconsistent with our overriding

1. Reciprocity is the exchange of something between people or groups of people when each person or group gives or allows something to the other. * They gave assurances they would press for reciprocity with Greece in the issuing of visas.
2. If something bodes ill, it makes you think that something bad will happen in the future. If something bodes well, it makes you think that something good will happen.

loyalties to the world organization? I reply that, on the contrary, it is probably the only means by which that organization will achieve its full stature and strength. There are already the special United States relations with Canada which I've just mentioned, and there are the relations between the United States and the South American Republics. We have also—We British have also our twenty years Treaty of Collaboration and Mutual Assistance with Soviet Russia. I agree with Mr. Bevin, the Foreign Secretary of Great Britain, that it might well be a fifty years treaty so far as we are concerned. We aim at nothing but mutual assistance and collaboration with Russia. We have an alliance—The British have an alliance with Portugal unbroken since the year 1384, and which produced fruitful results at a critical moment in the—in the recent war. None of these clash with the general interest of a world agreement, or a world organization; on the contrary, they help it. "In my father's house are many mansions." Special associations between members of the United Nations which have no aggressive point against any other country, which harbor no design incompatible with the Charter of the United Nations, far from being harmful, are beneficial and, as I believe, indispensable.

I spoke earlier, ladies and gentlemen, of—of the Temple of peace. Workmen from all countries must build that temple. If two of the workmen know each other particularly well and are old friends, if their families are intermingled, if they have "faith in each other's purpose, hope in each other's future and charity towards each other's shortcomings[1]"—to quote some good words I read here the other day —why cannot they work together at the common task as friends and partners? Why can they not share their tools and thus increase each other's working powers? Indeed they must do so or else the temple may not be built, or, being built, it may collapse, and we should all be proved again unteachable and have to go and try to learn again for a third time in a school of war incomparably more rigorous than that from which we have just been released. The dark ages may return, the Stone Age may return on the gleaming wings of science, and

1. Someone's or something's shortcomings are the faults or weaknesses which they have.

what might now shower immeasurable material blessings upon mankind, may even bring about its total destruction. Beware, I say; time may be short. Do not let us take the course of allowing events to drift along until it is too late. If there is to be a fraternal association of the kind of I have described, with all the express strength and security which both our countries can derive from it, let us make sure that that great fact is known to the world, and that it plays its part in steadying and stabilizing the foundations of peace. There is the path of wisdom. Prevention is better than the cure.

*A shadow has fallen upon the scenes so lately light by the Allied victory. *Nobody knows what Soviet Russia and its Communist international organization intends to do in the immediate future, or what are the limits, if any, to their expansive and proselytizing[1] tendencies. I have a strong admiration and regard for the valiant Russian people and for my wartime comrade, Marshall Stalin. There—There is deep sympathy and goodwill in Britain—and I doubt not here also—towards the peoples of all the Russias and a resolve to persevere through many differences and rebuffs in establishing lasting friendships. We understand the Russian need to be secure on her western frontiers by the removal of all possibility of German aggression. We welcome Russia to her rightful place among the leading nations of the world. We welcome her flag upon the seas. Above all, we welcome, or should welcome, constant, frequent, and growing contacts between the Russian people and our own peoples on both sides of the Atlantic. It is my duty however, for I am sure you would not wish me to not misstate the... facts as I see them to you. It is my duty to place before you certain facts about the present position in Europe.

From Stettin in the Baltic to Trieste in the Adriatic an iron curtain has descended across the Continent. Behind that line lie all the capitals of the ancient states of Central and Eastern Europe. Warsaw, Berlin, Prague, Vienna, Budapest, Belgrade,

1. If you proselytize, you try to persuade someone to share your beliefs, especially religious or political beliefs.

Bucharest and Sofia, all these famous cities and the populations around them lie in what I must call the Soviet sphere, and all are subject in one form or another, not only to Soviet influence but to a very high and, in some cases, increasing measure of control from—from Moscow. Athens alone—Greece with its immortal glories—is free to decide its future at an election under British, American, and French observation. The Russian-dominated Polish government has been encouraged to make enormous and wrongful inroads upon Germany, and mass expulsions of millions of Germans on a scale grievous and undreamed-of are now taking place. The Communist parties, which were very small in all these Eastern States of Europe, have been raised to preeminence and power far beyond their numbers and are seeking everywhere to obtain totalitarian control. Police governments are prevailing in nearly every case, and so far, except in Czechoslovakia, there is no true democracy.

Turkey and Persia are both profoundly alarmed and disturbed at the claims which are being made upon them and at the pressure being exerted by the Moscow government. An attempt is being made by the Russians in Berlin to build up a quasi-Communist party in their zone of occupied Germany by showing special favors to groups of left-wing German leaders. At the end of the fighting last June, the American and British armies withdrew westward, in accordance with an earlier agreement, to a depth at some points of 150 miles upon a front of nearly four hundred miles, in order to allow our Russian allies to occupy this vast expanse of territory which the Western democracies had conquered.

If now the Soviet government tries, by separate action, to build up a pro-Communist Germany in their areas, this will cause new serious difficulties in the America and British zones, and will give the defeated Germans the power of putting themselves up to[1] auction between the Soviets and the Western

1. If you put someone up to something wrong or foolish or something which they would not normally do, you suggest that they do it and you encourage them to do it. • How do you know he asked me out? You put him up to

democracies. Whatever conclusion may be drawn from these facts—and facts they are—this is certainly not the liberated Europe we fought to build up. Nor is it one which contains the essentials of permanent peace.

The safety of the world, ladies and gentleman, requires a new unity in Europe, from which no nation should be permanently outcast. it is from the quarrels of the strong parent races in Europe that the world wars we have witnessed, or which occurred in former times, have sprung. Twice in our own lifetime we have seen the United States, against their wishes and their traditions, against arguments, the force of which it is impossible - the force of which it is impossible not to comprehend. Twice we have seen them drawn by irresistible forces into these wars in time to secure the victory of the good cause, but only after frightful slaughter and devastation have occurred. Twice the United States has had to send several millions of its young men across the Atlantic to find the war; but now war can find any nation, wherever it may dwell between dusk and dawn. Surely we should work with conscious purpose for a grand pacification of Europe, within the structure of the United Nations and in accordance with our Charter. That, I feel, is - opens a course of policy of very great importance.

In front of the iron curtain which lies across Europe are other causes for anxiety. In Italy the Communist Party is seriously hampered by having to support the Communist-trained Marshal Tito's claims to former Italian territory at the head of the Adriatic. Nevertheless, the future of Italy hangs in the balance. Again one cannot imagine a regenerated Europe without a strong France. All my public life I worked for a strong France, and I never lost faith in her destiny, even in the darkest hours. I will not lose faith now. However, in a great number of countries, far from the Russian frontiers and throughout the world, Communist fifth columns[1] are established and work in complete unity and absolute

1. fifth column : a group of people who act traitorously and subversively out of a secret sympathy with an enemy of their country.

obedience to the directions they receive from the Communist center. Except in the British Commonwealth and in the United States where Communism is in its infancy, the Communist parties or fifth columns constitute a growing challenge and peril to Christian civilization. These are somber facts for anyone to have recite on the morrow a victory gained by so much splendid comradeship in arms and in the cause of freedom and democracy; but we should be most unwise not to face them squarely[1] while time remains.

The outlook is also anxious in the Far East and especially in Manchuria. The Agreement which was made at Yalta, to which I was a party, was extremely favorable to Soviet Russia, but it was made at a time when no one could say that the German war might not extend all through the summer and autumn of 1945 and when the Japanese war was expected by the best judges to last for a further 18 months from the end of the German war. In this country you all so well-informed about the Far East, and such devoted friends of China, that I do not need to expatiate on the situation there.

I have, however, felt bound to portray the shadow which, alike in the west and in the east, falls upon the world. I was a minister at the time of the Versailles Treaty and a close friend of Mr. Lloyd-George, who was the head of the British delegation at Versailles. I did not myself agree with many things that were done, but I have a very strong impression in my mind of that situation, and I find it painful to contrast it with that which prevails now. In those days there were high hopes and unbounded confidence that the wars were over and that the League of Nations would become all-powerful. I do not see or feel that same confidence or even the same hopes in the haggard world at the present time.

On the other hand, ladies and gentlemen, I repulse the idea that a new war is inevitable—still more that it is imminent. It is

1. If you face something squarely, you face it directly, without trying to avoid it. • The management committee have faced the situation squarely.

because I am sure that our fortunes are still in our own hands and that we hold the power to save the future, that I feel the duty to speak out now that I have the occasion[1] and the opportunity to do so. I do not believe that Soviet Russia desires war. What they desire is the fruits of war and the indefinite expansion of their power and doctrines. But what we have to consider here today while time remains, is the permanent prevention of war and the establishment of conditions of freedom and democracy as rapidly as possible in all countries. Our difficulties and dangers will not be removed by closing our eyes to them. They will not be removed by mere waiting to see what happens; nor will they be removed by a policy of appeasement. What is needed is a settlement, and the longer this is delayed, the more difficult it will be and the greater our dangers will become.

From what—what I have seen of our Russian friends and Allies during the war, I am convinced that there is nothing they admire so much as strength. And there is nothing for which they have less respect than for weakness, especially military weakness. For that—For that reason the old doctrine of a balance of power is unsound. We cannot afford, if we can help it, to work on narrow margins, offering temptations to a trial of strength. If the Western democracies stand together in strict adherence to the principles of the United Nations Charter there influence for furthering those principles will be immense and no one is likely to molest them. If, however, they become divided or falter in their duty, and if these all-important years are allowed to slip away, then indeed catastrophe may overwhelm us all.

Last time I saw it all coming and I cried aloud to my own fellow countrymen and to the world, but—but no one paid any attention. Up till the year 1933 or even 1935, Germany might have been saved from the awful fate which has overtaken her, and we might all have been spared the miseries Hitler let loose upon mankind. There never was a war in history easier to prevent by timely action than the one which has just desolated

1. An occasion for doing something is an opportunity for doing it. • It is an occasion for all the family to celebrate.

such great areas of the globe. It could have been prevented in my belief without the firing of a single shot, and Germany might be powerful, prosperous, and honored today; but no one would listen and one by one we were all sucked into the awful whirlpool. We surely, ladies and gentleman, I put it to you, surely, we must not let that happen again. This can only be achieved by reaching now, in 1946 - this year, 1946 - by reaching a good understanding on all points with Russia under the general authority of the United Nations Organization and by the maintenance of that good understanding through many peaceful years, by the World Instrument, supported by the whole strength of the English-speaking world and all its connections. There is the solution which I respectfully offer to you in this address to which I have given the title, "The Sinews of Peace."

Let—Let no man underrate[1] the abiding power of the British Empire and - and Commonwealth. Because you see - Because you see the 46millions in our island harassed about their food supply, of which they only grow one half, even in war-time, or because we have difficulty in restarting our industries and export trade after six years of passionate war effort, do not suppose we shall not come through these dark years of privation as we have come through the glorious years of agony. Do not suppose that half a century from now you will not see 70 or 80 millions of Britons spread about the world united in defense of our traditions, and our way of life, and of the world causes which you and we espouse. If - If the population of the English-speaking Commonwealths be added to that of the United States with all that such cooperation implies in the air, on the sea, all over the globe, and in science, and in industry, and in moral force, there will be no quivering, precarious balance of power to offer its temptation to ambition or adventure. On the contrary, there will be an overwhelming assurance of security. If we adhere faithfully to the Charter of the United Nations and walk forward in sedate and sober strength seeking no one's land or treasure, seeking to

1. If you underrate someone or something, you do not recognize how clever, important, or significant they are. • We women have a lot of good business skills, although we tend to underate ourselves.

lay no arbitrary control upon the thoughts of men; if all British moral and material forces and convictions are joined with your own in fraternal association, the highroads[1] of the future will be clear, not only for us, but for all; not only for our times, but for a century to come.

1. If you describe someone or something as sedate, you mean that they are quiet and rather dignified, though perhaps a bit dull.

AFTER YOU READ

1. According to Churchill, what is our supreme task and duty?

2. He has now stated war and tyranny. What are in many cases the prevailing anxiety?

3. If the dangers of war and tyranny are removed, what can science and cooperation certainly bring in the next few decades to the world?

4. The sure prevention of war, and the continuous rise of world organization will be gained with ______________________________.

5. Churchill referred to an iron curtain first. Would you explain it in detail?

6. To prevent soviet expansion of power and doctrines, what do we have to consider here today?

17

TWO BATHS

Elizabeth Graver

I was, at this first bath, twenty, spending the year studying in France, but traveling for a week with an American friend in Germany. Why Germany? Because it was cheap, because my eye landed on it as I sat in Chartres[1] in the Bibliothèque André-Malraux and stared at an enormous atlas; because I like the name Baden-Baden—the way it repeated on the tongue and meant Bath-Bath.

For a few days we had been walking in the outer fringes of the Black Forest, a landscape that reminded me of the New England mountains where I grew up—the same gentle shapes and deep pine colors, only here you could eat rich, dark cake in cafes, pour tea from iron kettles with acorns on their lids, climb wooden lookouts[2] on the trails and sleep in clean youth hostels where Canadians planted flags on their night tables, lest someone mistake them for Americans.

We were Americans though we bore no flags, privileged young women traveling on our parents' money. We were dark and funny, a comedy team, eager to talk to strangers, quick to hitch a ride from a man in a black turtleneck, black jeans, and black Mercedes. A count, I remember imagining as I sat in the back seat. He might take us home to his castle. He might wine and dine us. Or rape us. The thoughts slid calmly across my mind and disappeared.

---

1. Chartres: 프랑스 북부, 파리 서남쪽 도시
2.. lookouts: 망루

We were also Jewish, a fact that kept lighting my head in flashes. I tried to ignore in the train, for instance, as we rode precisely from one town to the next; in the way something in me curdled[1] when I heard the German language, my ears unable to find music there, though I knew all words held music if you listened right. I hadn't come to Germany for history, but it kept prodding me. I found that in this country I, always a bit outside myself, was even more outside, looking, looking[2] at myself— my black hair, fair skin, long nose, long face: can they tell, is it obvious? And how weak and skinny I felt there, next to the strapping[3] couple who ran the cafe we sat in for hours—a man and a woman as tall, blond, and leggy as giraffes.

We went to the baths to relax after days of walking in the Black Forest. Like two girls in a tale, we climbed the marble steps, clutching money whose worth we didn't know how to tally, walking into a palace where we didn't quite belong. Our clothes were sweaty and dirty from days of traveling. My hair was pulled back with a purple shoelace; my friend's hair was cropped close to her head like a boy's. I felt far from home and wanted a bath the way a child does—for its cradling water, the lathering of my skin, the flipping of my head into capable hands. I wanted heat, too, for it was late November and We'd been cold in the mountains. We paid our marks and went inside.

Where I saw, at first, nothing but beauty: tiles were covered green peacocks, beaded with water: damp white floors and high windows; rooms leading, maze like, one into another, each room with its own clean purpose—salty or steamy, hot, cold, or in-between. There were signs on the walls but we couldn't read them; we moved by our senses, from here to there. In the first room, stripping our clothes, I remember stretching and feeling small and puny, and (somehow, at the same time) firm and lucky. Next to me, my friend unhooked her bra, stepped out of her underpants, taller than I was, a bit rounder, and on her hip (unseen, as of yet,

1. curdle: (피) 등이 응고되다
2. If you prod someone or something, you give them a quick push with your finger or with a pointed object.
3. If you describe someone as strapping, you mean that they are tall and strong, and look healthy.

by her parents) the blurry tattoo of a blue rose.

Looking back, I know I must have had the body of a girl—the flat stomach and smooth thighs of a twenty-year-old who'd had an easy life and never given birth. All around us old European women bent over their long breasts, soaped at their wrinkled skin, sat on benches and ribbed pumice[1] stones along the tired soles of their feet. So much skin, I remember thinking, so much loose flesh, and I wanted and did not want to look, feeling my own flesh as so firm, so new, and yet knowing at the same time that I might be witnessing a vision of my future. Time, in this bath, came to me as a folded, pleated thing, and I recognized that, before I knew it, I'd be thirty looking back (as indeed, now, I am), and then forty looking back, and then it came to me (standing there so far from home, my pores yawning open) that even if I were lucky enough to live a long life, one day I would die.

It came to me, perhaps, because the steam blurred things so that the edges of bodies almost disappeared and matter came apart along its seams. There I was, surrounded by strangers, each one naked, touching her own skin. I wanted a towel or a skirt, but the women around me seemed utterly unselfconscious, even as they were covered with the nicks[2] and marks of age. Everywhere I looked I saw bareness—the sharp angle of an elbow, the dip of a breast, the dark line between buttocks—women with bodies, concentrating on themselves. Naked the way animals are, I thought, and I watched a squat[3] woman bend over and scrub between her legs like monkey cleaning itself.

And then a flash again, a vision on the outer fringes of my mind: here we were, my friend and I, in a bath where we couldn't read the signs. And at any moment the gas would came in, invisible as air, and we would crumble, draw our last breaths, and who was to say what the woman in the white dress like a nurse's costume wanted with us? Who could decipher the language,

1. A pumice stone is a piece of pumice that you rub over your skin in order to clean the skin or make it smoother.
2. A nick is a small cut made in the surface of something, usually in someone's skin.
3. If you describe someone or something as squat, you mean they are short and thick, usually in an unattractive way.

rough and throaty[1] as a dog's bark, that sprang from her throat as we pass by?

Cover yourself, I thought. And yet here I was, a tourist, having willingly paid my money, shed[2] my clothes. Don't be paranoid[3], I told myself. Don't make these people pay for their ancestors' crimes. But for an airless moment I couldn't look at the clean white ceiling, the hard white walls, without seeing the texture of bleached bone.

Then we were in the next room, lying each of us, face down on benches built into the edges of a large stone structure like a pyramid with steps. And before I could protest or question, another woman in a nurse's uniform was leaning over me with a loofah[4] sponge.

I want to leave, I thought. Please let me go. The sponge was hurting me, and I hadn't signed up for this, but here she was touching me, leaning over me like a surgeon, taking off my skin. I lay on my stomach, my teeth gritted, my muscles clenched, feeling the stone hard beneath my hipbones, breasts, and cheek. When she was done, she tapped me on my back and showed me the loofah mitt and my own arm—both covered with limp, gray threads of skin.

"*Ja*?" she said, and I nodded, smiled weakly, and looked for my friend, who was under the mitt of another woman, only she was laughing, calling out Nein nein, and the mitt woman was laughing too and roughly batting at my friend.

I'm not sure how long we spent in the bath in Baden-Baden; time grew heavy[5] as a towel soaked in water. I know we stayed longer than we should have, determined to get our money's worth. We lingered long enough so that we suddenly found ourselves walking, dazed into a room filled with both men and women, the men looking up at us, perhaps forty pairs of eyes, twenty penises,

---

1. A throaty voice or laugh is low and rather rough(=hoarse)
2. shed: 옷을 벗어버리다
3. If you say that someone is paranoid, you mean that they are extremely suspicious and afraid of other people.
4. A loofah is a long rough sponge-like piece of plant fiber which you use to scrub your body
5. grew heavy: 매우 따분하다

most of them old and shriveled in the water. Laughter struck me, then; something like mirth or discomfort or both cramped my stomach. Only later did someone tell us that at four o'clock the bath became mixed. Mixed, I remember thinking: men and women, Jews and Christian, Germans and foreigners, our skin and theirs, everyone only half pretending not to look.

"Are you twins?" an old woman asked us in English as we sank into the water.

We giggled and shook our heads. Twins? Why would we be twins? My friend was a good four inches taller than I was, my eyes hazel[1], hers brown, our bodies not at all the same shape.

What she means, I thought, is: Are you Jews? Then I kicked myself[2] for my assumptions. You're paranoid, I told myself again, and I remembered how the mother of a childhood friend posted a picture of children in a concentration camp on her family's gleaming fridge, to remind her daughters of how lucky they were and how unlucky their history was—a strange mixed message that left her family reeling[3]. Her girls could not eat, starved themselves, binged[4] and purged inside the mansion where they lived with a mother who read books about the Holocaust each night before bed.

"It's all right," my grandmother said to my mother when, as a girl, she shattered an eggshell-blue teacup made in Japan. "There goes another Jap!"

At the end of our hours in the bath, a woman with strong arms came up and cocooned us in white sheets until, hemmed in, we couldn't move our arms and could walk only by taking baby steps along the polished floor. She gestured, then, at a huge circular room with cots arranged around its edge, and we minced along until we reached two metal cots. To lie down we had to

1. Hazel eyes are greenish-brown in colour. 엷은 갈색
2. You use kick yourself in expression such as I could have kicked myself and you're going to kick yourself to indicate that you were annoyed or are going to be annoyed that you got something wrong.
3. If someone reels, they move about in an unsteady way as if they are going to fall.
4. If you binge, you do too much of something, such as drinking alcohol, eating, or spending money.

flop ourselves backward all in one motion, and then there we were, blanketed and snug as infants, trapped and held as prisoners, flat on our backs in an elegant white room where the light slanted down through a high dome and steam wafted through the door and all around us strangers slept. There we were, limbs tied, hungry now and dizzy and slipping toward something like mirth.

When the laughter came, it was sharp and hard and brought us close to gagging, for we couldn't sit up, quite, or get out from our wrappings. Inside our laughter lived too many things to describe: our own lightheartedness, certainly (the heat, the water, hours without food), but also a thick, teary sense of how hard it was to fix on[1] anything in this place so far from home—a place where women who cleaned us like mothers reminded us of gas chambers; where we stepped outside ourselves and saw our bodies in their youth and in their death; where we were not quite sure if we were being coddled[2] or choked.

"Shhh," I said to my friend, which only made her laugh harder. From other cots, people turned their heads and glared at us. And then a nurse-woman stomped in, frowned, unwrapped us, and sent us out to where our clothes lay waiting.

Later that afternoon, we met an old woman on a bus and she took us home for tea and showed us pictures of her family—men in SS uniforms with swastikas[3] embroidered on their hats.

"*Sehr* handsome, *ja*?" she said, pointing at the men, and we nodded and prodded each other under the table.

Her house was small and made of stone, her food simple. Her legs were stocky and her laughter nervous. I knew she wanted something from us, but I could not tell what. For hours we sat there as she showed us her embroidery and photographs and spoke to us in streams of German we couldn't understand, mixed in with bits of English.

"Address telephone," she said at one point. "You und you."

---

1. If you fix on a particular thing, you decide that is the one you want and will have.
2. To coddle someone means to treat them too kindly or protect them too much.
3. A swastikas is a symbol in the shape of a cross with each arm bent over at right angles. It is used in India as a good luck sign, but it was also used by the Nazis in Germany as their official symbol.

Dutifully, we wrote them down.

"Und America," she said when she saw I'd written my address in Paris, so I wrote down my parents' address as well.

"Stay," she commanded when it grew dark and we got up to leave. "Stay stay stay!" she stood and flapped her arms up and down like a plump, anxious bird or a child winding up for a tantrum[1].

"No," we said nervously, "no, but thank you, *danke*."

She flew into a panic then, ran around the house collecting things in a basket to send off with us: a red glass cup, a piece of lace, sausages, bread, a spool of thread.

"No," we said, "don't give us all that, really."

But she pressed the basket into our hands.

That night at the youth hostel, I peered into the mirror in the bathroom and wondered what she'd seen. Who was this woman who charged[2] over to us in the bus and took us home as if she'd been waiting for months for our arrival? Why was she giving us things? Why had she shown us her relatives but ignored the swastikas on their hats?

Uncomfortably, I saw pieces of my self in her—in her longing and frenzy, her desire to take strangers home, collect objects in a basket, comb over photographs pointing out only what she wanted to see. In her effort, especially, to find, in the world of daily things, small footholds of meaning, a place to rest. And then I saw her relatives again in their uniforms, and my own face which may or may not have announced me as Jewish, my skin taut and open from the bath. Perhaps what she was saying was quite simple: Look—my people, the faces I love. Handsome, *ja*? Or maybe she was saying, Yes, here are my relatives who were Nazis, but years have passed and I'd like to feed you now. Whatever she wanted me to see, I know I could see only one thing: men made faceless by the overbearing symbols on their hats.

After we left (I later found out), she picked up her phone and

1. If a child has a tantrum, they lose their temper in a noisy and uncontrolled way. If you say that an adult is throwing a tantrum, you are criticizing them for losing their temper and acting in a childish way.
2. If you charge towards someone or something, you move quickly and aggressively towards them.

placed a call to my parents overseas. When they answered, she said, "Daughter, *wunderbar*," and my parents panicked, knowing only that I was traveling, thinking I might be hurt, or dead. For months after I got back to Paris, I received post cards from her, written in German, signed with hearts and smiles. I never answered, too unsure of what she wanted. War guilt, said my French friends. After a while, the postcards stopped.

Did the woman from Baden-Baden ever ride the bus to the baths, untie her brown shoes, take off her thick wool skirt, unpeel her stockings, and sit on a bench, hosed in her own body, her own flesh, still with herself for a moment? Did she always scan the bus for strangers to take home—girls to mother, Jews or American to look at her photographs, mouths to feed, ears that could hear her sounds but not begin to understand? War guilt, perhaps (could she tell we were Jewish?), but I think that's only one part of the picture. Really I have no idea who I was to that woman, and I cannot describe in any simple way who she was to me. I know I felt scrubbed and naked that afternoon, missing a layer of skin. She tried to give me gifts; I said no. Later she wrote to me; I didn't answer. Daughter *wunderwar.* A call from across the ocean. This is not a story I can make clearer. That night I slept clean, tired and slightly less sure of my place in the world.

2

And then I was thirty, and my mother was fifty-eight. For three weeks we had been traveling together in Turkey, the country where my mother's parents were born and grew up. On this, our last day, we had come to a *hamam*, a Turkish bath, down an alley in a gray, ordinary section of the city of Ankara. This building, unlike the bathhouse in Baden-Baden, was plain on the outside—beige stucco with a nicked brown door. Inside, we left our clothes in a small room with a key, put on plastic clogs[1], and walked into a huge marble chamber dense with steam. My mother was naked and, without her glasses, nearly blind. On this trip she had seemed

1. Clogs are heavy leather or wooden shoes with thick wooden soles.

both old and young to me—young as we met children and scrambled after them down hills[1], through tunnels, into abandoned churches; old in the deepening fan of lines around her eyes, the frailty of her shoulders, the way she told me she felt invisible when we walked down the street and the men called out to me: Pretty girl, come have tea, hello American girl!

I crouched in a corner on the floor, held a plastic jug under the spigots of squat marble sink, and poured hot and cold water over myself. I watched a Turkish woman lead my mother out across the floor. My mother groped forward, extended her foot to test for level ground. The woman took her firmly by her arm and laid her down across the *gobek tasi*, or navel stone—an octagonal marble platform in the middle of the room. Above it, a dome rose like a pregnant belly, studded with round windows. From here (I, too, without my glasses, the world a little blurry) I might have been looking at a painting: two women in a bath, my mother and a stranger, their skin steamed and rosy in the light that filtered through the windows in the roof. My mother might have been a woman my own age, or this might have been not Ankara but Istanbul, where my grandmother used to visit the baths.

For Muslims, I had read, running water has mystical properties. And for jews? For my Sephardic[2] grandmother? Sitting in the halflight of the bath, I pictured my grandmother as a first-time bride in Istanbul. Her name before she was married the first name was Rebecca Cohen; then Rebecca Baruch, and later Rebecca Levy, like a spell with three parts. Like the Muslims, the Jews in Turkey sent the bride to the *hamam* for a ritual bath before her wedding. My grandmother would have been around nineteen the year she married Moses Baruch, a man who she told me (in the winding stories she spun the year before she died) worked in a cheese factory. I've seen a picture of her at this age, and it must be said that she was unusually beautiful, with a strong chin, a proud gaze, thick eyebrows, and luxuriant[3], wavy brown hair.

---

1. If you scramble over rocks or up a hill, you move quickly over them or up it using your hands to help you
2. Sephardic: 스페인, 포르투칼 유태인의, 또 그 자손의; 주로 의식, 종교적 습관 및 헤브라이어의 발음에 의해서 유럽중동부계 유태인과 구별된다.
3. If you describe someone's hair luxuriant, you mean that it is very thick and

Two days before my grandmother's wedding, she would have had her hair, hands, and nails dyed red with henna[1] sent by her groom, Moses, on a copper tray rimmed with candles. Her family would have rented the whole *hamam* for her ritual bath, or if they couldn't afford to rent the whole place, they would have used the Jewish corner. My grandmother's mother would have gone with her, along with her sisters, her aunts, her friends, perhaps even her close friend Suzanne Behar, who would later become the first wife of my grandfather Samuel Levy, the man my grandmother would marry after Moses Baruch and Suzanne Behar both died. In the bath, my grandmother, her sisters, mother, friends and aunts would strip off their clothes and chatter in Ladino—the archaic Spanish spoken by Sephardic Jews. Or they would sing, perhaps, in Turkish, Ladino, or French. I can picture my grandmother at the center of it all, gulping down the attention[2], singing the loudest, arching her body down onto the navel stone in the middle of the hamam. Was she scared that day, smeared[3] with henna the color of dried blood, preparing her body for sex? If she was, I doubt she showed it; my grandmother had a talent for disguise.

She would have brought a package with her, a *bogo de banyo* from her future husband. The gift would have arrived wrapped in fabric embroidered with artichokes and tulips—a cloth valued for its reversibility[4], perfect inside and out with nothing to hide, like a good wife. Inside, a set of towels to cover the shoulders, the head, the torso. Also a lasa de banyo—a brass bowl for rinsing the body; and wooden clogs inlaid with mother-of-pearl; and combs, soaps, and perfumes; and money to pay for the bath.

Before my grandmother's ritual immersion, the women throw sugar cubes in the water. For a sweet life, Rebecca. (Would her life turn out sweet? Much bitterness and loss inside it; spurts of laughter, too) She squats, tips her head back, and they cluster

---

healthy

1. henna: 헤나 염료; 적갈색; 부처 꽃과의 관목
2. gulping down the attention: 사람들의 주목을 받으며
3. If you smear a surface with an oily or sticky substance or smear the substance onto the surface, you spread a layer of the substance over the surface.
4. reversibility: 양면겸용의; 안팎이 같은 천

around and douse[1] her with water from the sink. As she stands up, someone (her mother? her sister?) breaks a yeast cake over her. A blessing. To life. To children (she will bear five). And with a giggle, some knowing looks, and a slap on the behind: to love.

I remembered my grandmother with her Jean Naté bath splash, and how, in her last days, when she had one leg and spoke in a torrent of Ladino, French, English and Turkish, she still loved a good bath, the towels plumped and flesh, her Avon products left over from her days as an Avon lady in Florida, when she charmed her customers with songs. I remembered how exacting she was when she taught me to embroider; the cloth had to look as good on its underside as on its top. At home my parents keep matchbooks in a brass dish my grandfather said was for scooping water at the bath. A disgusting place, he said, drawing out the syllables—*deee-scoost-sting.* Unclean, where bad things happened. Later I learned from my mother that my grandfather's brother was gay and frequented the baths in Istanbul, bringing shame on the family.

My grandfather, as I remember him, was strict, practical, and wary of pleasure; it was hard to imagine him here. But my grandmother loved bodies, her own and other people's. As I watched my mother being bathed, I remembered the day, as a child, that I looked under my grandmother's couch pillows for drawing paper (everything tucked away and hidden in her house) and found, instead, calendar foldouts[2] of naked women, plump, pink, and glistening, and how she laughed and mock-slapped me when I held them up.

"Don't be ashamed," she said, "of a person's body. It's a beautiful thing. What you think you're doing looking in that couch, you? You give me those, you wise guy! *Bee yooo-tee-ful,* her voice prancing[3] up and down.

I watched my mother lying on the marble, her body so much

---

1. If you douse someone or something with a liquid, you throw a lot of that liquid over them.
2. calender foldouts: 접어 넣은 달력의 페이지들
3. If someone prances around, they walk or move around with exaggerated movements, usually because they want people to look at them and admire them.(껑충거리며 걷다)

like mine except that her stomach was rounder, her nipples darker, for she'd lived twenty-eight years longer than I and had given birth twice. The water as I poured over myself was either too cold or too hot, but the marble was gray-veined and smooth and I crouched in my corner and listen to women speak in a rising, falling melody I couldn't understand. During our three weeks in this country where almost everyone was Muslim, we'd seen mostly women beneath veils, hanging back in doorways or courtyards. Here the bathing women were naked, and the staff wore tiny bikini underwear and wet brassieres. Watching them chat and drink tea from fluted glasses, I glimpsed how little I knew of the lives of anyone here, how much went on beneath veils, behind doors and windows.

And then my mother was being led back to our sink, and I was being led out to the navel stone, and a woman with a cheerful face and beige lace bra was leaning over me, scrubbing me roughly with her loofah mitt.

With my eyes shut, I might have been twenty years old in Baden-Baden; this might have been a woman in nurse's uniform; they had the same strong hands. Or I might have been four years old, this woman my mother or grand-mother, for she was scrubbing me as hard as if I were coated in playground grime and she had no shame, working over my breasts, down my belly, pushing apart my thighs so she could slide her mitt between my legs.

I did not protest, not even to myself. I had no visions, here, of water turning to gas. This was the country that had welcomed my ancestors when Spain expelled them in 1492 and had taken in thousands of Jews during the Holocaust. At twenty, I'd gone to Germany because the train fare was cheap and I was in the neighborhood, but I'd come to Turkey looking for something like recognition or knowledge, home or safety; this was, after all, a place I was linked to in my blood. Was it fair to feel that history as I barely skimmed the surface of a country for three weeks? I couldn't help it; I saw my grandfather's hooded[1] brown eyes in the eyes of a shopkeeper in the Grand Bazaar, saw my mother's

1. If someone had hooded eyes, their eyelids almost look as though they are partly closed.(덮개 달린)

and my own face in the faces of the girls we met in the streets. I heard Hebrew rhythms, even, in the wails of the mosques' call to prayer and saw Stars of David carved on village walls.

Did it matter that Muslims also made use of the six-pointed star, so that origins were impossible to fix? Did it matter that I was cared for in Germany, taken into a stranger's home, given gifts? It would have been easier, less foggy, to experience the bath in Baden-Baden as a cold, efficient death-place, and the bath in Ankara—with its navel stone and pregnant roof—as a place of continuity and birth. But it wasn't like that. I may have imagined death as I lay swaddled like a baby in Baden-Baden, but I was thirty in Ankara and that much closer to actual death, threads of gray speeding prematurely through my hair. I was washed by a round woman who may have looked cheerful but was probably tired, doing her job. While we were in Turkey, two Dutch women were abducted by their bus driver, raped, then killed. And what of the country's history and present state—the Armenian genocide, and the fact that on our trip we didn't travel to Turkey's southeast corner because of what the tourist bureau called "trouble with the Kurds"?

When the woman finished washing me, she, like the German woman, held up the mitt to show me how pieces of myself were clinging to the loofah—a snake's skin, my own grubby debris. Then she left me alone and I lay on the navel stone distant from myself, a body shucked[1] of its husk, a mind far from its body. I wished, then, that my mother had her glasses on so she could see me lying as she had lain a few minutes before, as her mother had lain more than seventy years ago. In the distance I could feel my mother's presence, and my grandmother's. Could this be a link, some kind of echo—vexed[2] and inside my own head, perhaps, but an echo nonetheless? I wasn't sure. I lay there pressed against the stone of a country I could recognize only in fragments—a brass bowl, embroidery perfect on both sides, *borek* pastries like the ones my grandmother used to make, their edges frail and flaky as my own shed skin.

---

1. shucked: 벗겨진
2. If someone or something vexes you, they make you feel annoyed, puzzled, and frustrated.

AFTER YOU READ

1. Two girls were having a bath in Germany. The writer said to herself, "Don't be paranoid." Why did she say so?

2. She met an old woman on a bus and was invited to her house. The woman showed them pictures of her family. How did the writer feel?

3. The Jews in Turkey sent the bride to the bath before her wedding. For what?

4. What kind of person was the writer's grandfather?

5. While the writer was having a bath in Turkey, she had no visions of water turning to gas. why?

18
TWO GALLANTS

James Joyce

The grey warm evening of August had descended upon the city and a mild warm air, a memory of summer, circulated in the streets. The streets, shuttered for the repose of Sunday, swarmed with a gaily coloured crowd. Like illumined pearls the lamps shone from the summits of their tall poles upon the living texture[1] below which, changing shape and hue unceasingly, sent up into the warm grey evening air an unchanging unceasing murmur.

Two young men came down the hill of Rutland Square[2]. One of them was just bringing a long monologue to a close[3]. The other, who walked on the verge of the path and was at times obliged to step on to the road, owing to his companion's rudeness, wore an amused listening face. He was squat[4] and ruddy. A yachting cap was shoved far back from his forehead and the narrative to which he listened made constant waves of expression break forth over his face from the corners of his nose and eyes and mouth. Little jets of wheezing laughter followed one anther out of his convulsed body. His eyes, twinkling with cunning enjoyment, glanced at every moment towards his companion's face. Once or twice he rearranged the light waterproof[5] which he had slung over one

1. the living texture: 살아 움직이는 조직, 즉 앞에 나온 "a gaily coloured crowd"를 가리킴.
2. Rutland Square: 더블린 중동부에 있는 현재의 Parnell Square.
3. bring a long monologue to a close: 독백에 가까운 장광설을 끝내다.
4. squat: 땅달막한(ungracefully short or low and thick).
5. waterproof: 비옷, 우의.

shoulder in toreador fashion[1]. His breeches, his white rubber shoes and his jauntily slung waterproof expressed youth. But his figure fell into rotundity at the waist, his hair was scant and grey and his face, when the waves of expression had passed over it, had a ravaged look.

When he was quite sure that the narrative had ended he laughed noiselessly for fully half a minute. Then he said;

—Well!... That takes the biscuit![2]

His voice seemed winnowed of vigour; and to enforce his words he added with humor;

—That takes the solitary, unique, and, if I may so call it, *recherche*[3] biscuit!

He became serious and silent when he had said this. His tongue was tired for he had been talking all the afternoon in a public-house[4] in Dorset Street[5]. Most people considered Lenehan a leech[6] but, in spite of this reputation, his adroitness and eloquence had always prevented his friends from forming any general policy against him. He had a brave manner of coming up to a party of them in a bar and of holding himself nimbly at the borders of the company until he was included in a round[7]. He was a sporting vagrant[8] armed with a vast stock of stories, limericks[9] and riddles. He was insensitive to all kinds of discourtesy. No one knew how he achieved the stern task of living, but his name was vaguely associated with racing tissues[10].

–And where did you pick her up, Corley? he asked.

Corley ran his tongue swiftly along his upper lip.

–One night, man, he said, I was going along Dame Street and

---

1. in toreador fashion: 투우사 모양으로.
2. That takes the biscuit.: "들어 본 중에서 최고다."(That is the best I have ever heard.) "take the biscuit(=the cake)": deserve a prize for excellence.
3. *recherche*: rare, in demand.(Fr.) *rechercher*(=seek)의 p.p.
4. public house: (경양식도 곁들여 파는) 술집. 흔히 "pub"이라고 한다.
5. Dorset Street: 더블린 중앙에서 북동쪽으로 뻗은 거리.
6. leech: 남의 등을 쳐 먹는 자(a blood-sucking worm, hence who sticks to other people to suck gain out of them.)
7. be included in a round : 술자리에 끼이다.
8. a sporting vagrant: 놀기 좋아하는 부랑자(건달).
9. limerick: 五行俗謠
10. racing tissues: 경마의 비밀정보(tip sheets or racing forms)

I spotted a fine tart[1] under Waterhouse's[2] clock and said good-night, you know. So we went for a walk round by the canal and she told me she was a slavey[3] in a house in Baggot Street[4]. I put my arm round her and squeezed her a bit that night. Then next Sunday, man, I met her by appointment. We went out to Donnybrook[5] and I brought her into a field there. She told me she used to go with a dairyman. . . . It was fine, man. Cigarettes every night she'd bring me and paying the tram out and back. And one night she brought me two bloody[6] fine cigars-O, the real cheese[7], you know, that the old fellow used to smoke.... I was afraid, man, she'd get in the family way[8]. But she's up to the dodge[9].

–Maybe she thinks you'll marry her, said Lenehan.

–I told her I was out of a job, said Corley. I told her I was in Pim's[10]. She doesn't know my name. I was too hairy[11] to tell her that. But she thinks I'm a bit of class[12], you know.

Lenehan laughed again, noiselessly.

–Of all the good ones ever I heard, he said, that emphatically takes the biscuit.

Corley's stride acknowledged the compliment. The swing of his burly body made his friend execute[13] a few light skips from the path to the roadway and back again. Corley was the son of

---

1. tart: 품행이 나쁜 여자, 창녀(woman of loose morals ; a prostitute)
2. Waterhouse: Dame Street에 있는 금은방
3. slavey: 하녀(maid-of-all-work)
4. Baggot Street: 더블린 동남쪽의 번화가.
5. Donnybrook: 더블린에서 남쪽으로 2마일쯤 떨어져 있는 교외.
6. bloody: "무지무지하게, 지독하게" (infamously, murderously)란 뜻의 점잖지 못한 slang, *Dubliners*의 출판교섭이 시작되었을 때 출판사 측에서 이 말의 삭제를 요구하였으나 조이스는 이를 거절, 출판이 지연된 사유의 하나가 되었다.
7. the real cheese: 진짜배기(the real thing).
8. in the family way: pregnant.
9. up to the dodge: 피할 길을 알고 있다. 즉, "She knows how to avoid becoming pregnant."
10. Pim's: a large Quaker dry-goods store(포목상) in Dublin. (현재는 실직자이나 한때는 좋은 직장에 다녔음을 과시함.)
11. hairy: cautious, shrewd, clever, astute (slang).
12. class: superior quality, distinction (slang).
13. execute a few light skips...to the roadway: 인도에서 차도로 갑자기 몇 발자국 밀리다.

an inspector[1] of police and he had inherited his father's frame and gait. He walked with his hands by his sides, holding himself erect and swaying his head from side to side. His head was large, globular and oily; it sweated in all weathers; and his large round hat, set upon it sideways, looked like a bulb which had grown out of another. He always stared straight before him as if he were on parade and, when he wished to gaze after someone in the street, it was necessary for him to move his body from the hips. At present he was about town[2]. Whenever any job was vacant a friend was always ready to give him the hard word. He was often to be seen walking with policemen in plain clothes, talking earnestly. He knew the inner side of all affairs and was fond of delivering final judgments. He spoke without listening to the speech of his companions. His conversation was mainly about himself; what he had said to such a person and what such a person had said to him and what he had said to settle the matter. When he reported these dialogues he aspirated the first letter of his name after the manner of Florentines[3].

Lenehan offered his friend a cigarette. As the two young men walked on through the crowd Corley occasionally turned to smile at some of the passing girls but Lenehan's gaze was fixed on the large faint moon circled with a double halo. He watched earnestly the passing of the grey web of twilight across its face. At length he said;

–Well... tell me, Corley, I suppose you'll be able to pull it off[4] all right, eh?

Corley closed one eye expressively as an answer.

–Is she game for[5] that? asked Lenehan dubiously. You can never know women.

---

1. inspector: 경위(police officer of middle rank).
2. about town: 일정한 직업 없이 빈둥거리며 지내다(그러나, "법망에는 걸리지 않을 짓을 해서 먹고 산다"는 뜻이 암시되어 있다.)
3. aspirated... of Florentines: 이탈리아의 Florence 사람들이 "casa"(house)를 "hasa"로("h"음을 넣어) 발음했듯이 Corley도 자기 이름을 "Horley" 또는 "whorely"로 발음했다. (이렇게 뻐기는 것은 Corley의 하녀에 대한 "gallantry"와 Dante의 Beatrice에 대한 그것과를 ironic하게 대조시키려는 뜻이 있는 것 같다.)
4. pull off: 성공하다(succeed in a difficult attempt, such as a trick or crime).
5. game for~: 기꺼이 ~할, ~할 마음이 있는(willing). 하녀가 마음에 내켜 적극적으로 나오는가?의 뜻.

–She's all right, said Corley. I know the way to get around[1] her, man. She's a bit gone on[2] me.

–You're what I call a gay Lothario[3], said Lenehan. And the proper kind of a Lothario, too!

A shade of mockery relieved the servility of his manner. To save himself he had the habit of leaving his flattery open to the interpretation of raillery[4]. But Corley had not a subtle mind.

–There's nothing to touch a good slavey, he affirmed. Take my tip[5] for it.

–By one who has tried them all, said Lenehan.

–First I used to go with girls, you know said Corley, unbosoming[6]; girls off the South Circular[7]. I used to take them out, man, on the tram somewhere and pay the tram or take them to a band or a play at the theatre or buy them chocolate and sweets or something that way. I used to spend money on them right enough, he added, in a convincing tone, as if he were conscious of being disbelieved.

But Lenehan could well believe it; he nodded gravely.

–I know that game, he said, and it's a mug's game[8].

–And damn the thing I ever got out of it, said Corley.

–Ditto[9] here, said Lenehan.

–Only off of one of them, said Corley.

He moistened his upper lip by running his tongue along it. The recollection brightened his eyes. He too gazed at the pale disc of the moon, now nearly veiled, and seemed to meditate.

–She was... a bit of all right, he said regretfully.

He was silent again. Then he added;

---

1. get around=get round: 구워 삶다. 주무르다.(coax; find a way to deal with something to his advantage.
2. gone on: 홀딱 반한(be infatuated with).
3. gay Lothario: 난봉꾼(lady-killer; libertine).
4. leave his flattery...raillery: 그의 치렛말을 조롱으로 해석할 수 도 있게 한다.
5. Take my tip: Listen to my tip(=묘수, 비밀정보)
6. unbosoming: 흉금을 털어 놓으며(telling the secret feelings)
7. girls off the South Circular: The South Circular Road는 애인이 없는 중하류층 처녀들의 인기 있는 산책로였다.
8. a mug's game: (slang)얼간이 짓. "mug": (slang)stupid person; dupe.
9. ditto: "동감이야." (the same)

–She's on the turf[1] now. I saw her driving down Earl Street[2] one night with two fellows with her on a car.

–I suppose that's your doing, said Lenehan.

–There was others at her before me, said Corley philosophically.

This time Lenehan was inclined to disbelieve. He shook his head to and fro and smiled.

–You know you can't kid me, Corley, he said.

–Honest to God! said Corley. Didn't she tell me herself?

Lenehan made a tragic gesture.

–Base betrayer! he said.

As they passed along the railings of Trinity College, Lenehan skipped out into the road and peered up at the clock.

–Twenty after[3], he said.

–Time enough, said Corley. She'll be there all right. I always let her wait a bit.

Lenehan Laughed quietly.

–Ecod[4]! Corley, you know how to take them, he said.

–I'm up to all their little tricks, Corley confessed.

–But tell me, said Lenehan again, are you sure you can bring it off[5] all right? You know it's a ticklish[6] job. They're damn close on that point. Eh?... What?

His bright, small eyes searched his companion's face for reassurance. Corley swung his head to and fro as if to toss aside an insistent insect, and his brows gathered.

–I'll pull it off. he said. Leave it to me, can't you?

Lenehan said no more. He did not wish to ruffle his friend's temper, to be sent to the devil[7] and told that his advice was not wanted. A little tact was necessary. But Corley's brow was soon smooth again. His thoughts were running another way.

---

1. on the turf: 창녀짓을 하다(become a prostitute).
2. Earl Street: Liffey 강 북쪽의 더블린 중앙에 있는 거리. 여기서 한 블록 가량 서쪽에 홍등가가 있다.
3. Twenty after: 오후 7시 20분인 듯. 배경이 8월 말경이므로 보통 해는 7시경에 진다.
4. Ecod!: 젠장 맞을!(a mild oath)
5. bring off: accomplish successfully.
6. ticklish: needing special care and attention.
7. to be sent to the devil: 앞의 "He did not wish to"에 연결해 읽을 것. Lenehan은 Corley로부터 배척을 받기 싫었다는 뜻. "send~to the devil": ~을 쫓아 버리다.

–She's a fine decent tart, he said, with appreciation; that's what she is .

They walked along Nassau Street and then turned into Kildare[1] Street. Not far from the porch of the club[2] a harpist stood in the roadway, playing to a little ring of listeners. He plucked at the wires heedlessly, glancing quickly from time to time at the face of each new-comer and from time to time, wearily also, at the sky. His harp[3] too, heedless that her coverings[4] had fallen about her knees, seemed weary alike of the eyes of strangers and of her master's hands. One hand played in the bass the melody of *Silent, O Moyle*[5], while the other hand careered in the treble[6] after each group of notes. The notes of the air throbbed deep and full.

The two young men walked up the street without speaking, the mournful music following them. When they reached Stephen's Green they crossed the road. Here the noise of trams, the lights and the crowd released them from their silence.

–There she is! said Corley.

At the corner of Hume Street[7] a young woman was standing. She wore a blue dress and a white sailor hat[8]. She stood on the curbstone, swinging a sunshade[9] in one hand. Lenehan grew lively.

–Let's have a squint at her, Corley, He said.

Corley glanced sideways at his friend and an unpleasant grin appeared on his face.

–Are you trying to get inside[10] me? he asked.

–Damn it! said Lenehan boldly, I don't want an introduction. All I want is to have a look at her. I'm not going to eat her.

–O ... A look at her? said Corley, more amiably. Well ... I'll tell you what. I'll go over and talk to her and you can pass by.

---

1. Kildare Street: Nassau Street에서 스티븐 공원 북쪽으로 뻗은 거리.
2. the club: Kildare Street Club(친영파들이 잘 가는 고급 사교장)
3. harp: a traditional symbol of Ireland's glorious past.
4. her coverings: 하프의 덮개.
5. *Silent, O Moyle*: Thomas Moore의 *Irish Melodies*에 실린 "The song of Fionnuala"의 첫 행의 일부(조이스의 애창곡의 하나).
6. treble: 최고음부.
7. Hume Street: Stephen's Green East에 인접한 거리.
8. sailor hat: (여성도 쓰는)밀짚모자의 일종.
9. sunshade: 양산.
10. get inside: 훼방 놓다. <공굴리기 놀이(game of bowls)에서 나온 말.>

–Right! said Lenehan.

Corley had already thrown one leg over the chains when Lenehan called out;

–And after? Where will we meet?

–Half ten, answered Corley, bringing over his other leg.

–Where?

–Corner of Merrion Street. We'll be coming back.

–Work it all right now, said Lenehan in farewell.

Corley did not answer. He sauntered across the road[1] swaying his head from side to side. His bulk, his easy pace and the solid sound of his boots had something of the conqueror in them. He approached the young woman and, without saluting, began at once to converse with her. She swung her sunshade more quickly and executed half turns of her heels. Once or twice when he spoke to her at close quarters she laughed and bent her head.

Lenehan observed them for a few minutes. Then he walked rapidly along beside the chains to some distance and crossed the road obliquely. As he approached Hume Street corner he found the air heavily scented and his eyes made a swift anxious scrutiny of the young woman's appearance. She had her Sunday finery on. Her blue serge skirt was held at the waist by a belt of black leather. The great silver buckle of her belt seemed to depress the centre of her body, catching the light stuff of her white blouse like a clip. She wore a short black jacket with mother-of-pearl[2] buttons and a ragged black boa[3]. The ends of her tulle collarette [4]had been carefully disordered and a big bunch of red flowers was pinned in her bosom, stems upwards[5]. Lenehan's eyes noted approvingly her stout short muscular body. Frank rude health glowed in her face, on her fat red cheeks and in her unabashed blue eyes. Her features were blunt. She had broad nostrils, a straggling mouth which lay open in a contented leer, and two projecting front teeth. As he passed Lenehan took off his cap and,

1. the road: Stephen's Green East.
2. mother-of-pearl: 자개.
3. boa: 긴 모피 목도리.
4. tulle collarette: 튤 망사로 된 칼라.
5. stems upwards: 꽃대를 위로 향하게 꽃을 다는 것은 세련성의 결여를 나타낸다.(보통 아래쪽으로 향하게 단다.)

after about ten seconds, Corley returned a salute to the air. This he did by raising his hand vaguely and pensively changing the angle of position of his hat.

Lenehan walked as far as the Shelbourne Hotel[1] where he halted and waited. After waiting for a little time he saw them coming towards him and, when they turned to the right he followed them, stepping lightly in his white shoes, down one side of Merrion Square[2]. As he walked on slowly, timing his pace to theirs, he watched Corley's head which turned at every moment towards the young woman's face like a big ball revolving on a pivot. He kept the pair in view until he had seen them climbing the stairs of the Donnybrook tram; then he turned about and went back the way he had come.

Now that he was alone his face looked older. His gaiety seemed to forsake him and, as he came by the railings of the Duke's Lawn[3], he allowed his hand to run along them. The air which the harpist had played began to control his movements. His softly padded feet played the melody while his fingers swept a scale of variations idly along the railings after each group of notes.

He walked listlessly round Stephen's Green and then down Grafton Street. Though his eyes took note of many elements of the crowd through which he passed they did so morosely. He found trivial all that was meant to charm him and did not answer the glances which invited him to be bold. He knew that he would have to speak a great deal, to invent and to amuse, and his brain and throat were too dry for such a task. The problem of how he could pass the hours till he met Corley again troubled him a little. He could think of no way of passing them but to keep on walking. He turned to the left when he came to the corner of Rutland Square and felt more at ease in the dark quiet street, the sombre look of which suited his mood. He paused at last before the window of a poor-looking shop over which the words

1. Shelbourne Hotel : Kildare Street와 Stephen's Green North의 교차점에 있는 특급 관광호텔. <조이스 탄생 백주년 기념 국제 학술대회 때(1982) 연회가 여기서 열렸다.>
2. Merrion Square : 18세기 풍의 멋진 광장의 하나.
3. Duke's Lawn: Merrion Square West의 서쪽에 있는 잔디밭.

Refreshment Bar[1] were printed in white letters. On the glass of the window were two flying inscriptions: *Ginger Beer and Ginger Ale*[2]. A cut ham was exposed on a great blue dish while near it on a plate lay a segment of very light plum-pudding. He eyed this food earnestly for some time and then, after glancing warily up and down the street, went into the shop quickly.

He was hungry for, except some biscuits which he had asked two grudging curates[3] to bring him, he had eaten nothing since breakfast-time. He sat down at an uncovered wooden table opposite two work-girls and a mechanic. A slatternly[4] girl waited on him.

–How much is a plate of peas? he asked.

–Three halfpence[5], sir, said the girl.

–Bring me a plate of peas, he said, and a bottle of ginger beer.

He spoke roughly in order to belie his air of gentility for his entry had been followed by a pause of talk. His face was heated. To appear natural he pushed his cap back on his head and planted his elbows on the table. The mechanic and the two work-girls examined him point by point before resuming their conversation in a subdued voice. The girl brought him a plate of hot grocer's peas, seasoned with pepper and vinegar, a fork and his ginger beer. He ate his food greedily and found it so good that he made a note of the shop mentally. When he had eaten all the peas he sipped his ginger beer and sat for some time thinking of Corley's adventure. In his imagination he beheld the pair of lovers walking along some dark road; he heard Corley's voice in deep energetic gallantries and saw again the leer of the young woman's mouth. This vision made him feel keenly his own poverty of purse and spirit. He was tired of knocking about, of pulling the devil by the

---

1. *Refreshment Bar*: 싸구려 식당인 듯.
2. Ginger Beer and Ginger Ale: 둘 다 진저 에일(생강이 든 비 알코올성 청량음료). 이 둘을 나란히 써붙인 것은 제품 이름이 다르거나 아니면 전자가 후자보다 맛이 순하면서 색이 진한 차이가 있는 듯.
3. curate: bartender (Dublin slang)
4. slatternly: 단정치 못한 (dirty and untidy).
5. three halfpence: "plate of peas" (baked or boiled dried peas)가 빈털터리 Lenehan이 사먹을 수 있는 가장 싸고 배부른 음식이란 뜻이 들어 있다.

tail[1], of shifts and intrigues[2]. He would be thirty-one in November. Would he never get a good job? Would he never have a home of his own? He thought how pleasant it would be to have a warm fire to sit by and a good dinner to sit down to. He had walked the streets long enough with friends and with girls. He knew what those friends were worth: he knew the girls too. Experience had embittered his heart against the world. But all hope had not left him. He felt better after having eaten than he had felt before, less weary of his life, less vanquished in spirit. He might yet be able to settle down in some snug corner and love happily if he could only come across some good simple-minded girl with a little of the ready[3].

He paid twopence halfpenny to the slatternly girl and went out of the shop to begin his wandering again. He went into Capel Street and walked along towards the City hall. Then he turned into Dame Street. At the corner of George's Street he met two friends of his and stopped to converse with them. He was glad that he could rest from all his walking. His friends asked him had he seen Corely and what was the latest. He replied that he had spent the day with Corley. His friends talked very little. They looked vacantly after some figures in the crowd and sometimes made a critical remark. One said that he had seen Mac an hour before in Westmoreland Street. At this Lenehan said that he had been with Mac the night before in Egan's[4]. The young man who had seen Mac in Westmoreland Street asked was it true that Mac had won a bit over a billiard match. Lenehan did not know: he said that Holohan had stood them drinks in Egan's.

He left his friends at a quarter to ten and went up George's Street. He turned to the left at the City markets[5] and walked on into Grafton Street. The crowd of girls and young men had thinned and on his way up the street he heard many groups and couples bidding one another good-night. He went as far as the

---

1. pull the devil by the tail: 궁핍하게 지내다(be in financial difficulties).
2. shifts and intrigues: 권모술수.
3. the ready: (slang) 현금(ready cash).
4. Egan's: 술집 이름.
5. the City Markets: Great George Street South의 동쪽에 있는 거리.

clock of the College of Surgeons[1]: it was on the stroke of ten. He set off briskly along the northern side of the Green, hurrying for fear Corley should return too soon. When he reached the corner of Merrion Street he took his stand in the shadow of a lamp and brought out one of the cigarettes which he had reserved and lit it. He leaned against the lamp-post and kept his gaze fixed on the part from which he expected to see Corley and the young woman return.

His mind became active again. He wondered had Corley managed it successfully. He wondered if he had asked her yet or if he would leave it to the last. He suffered all the pangs and thrills of his friend's situation as well as those of his own. But the memory of Corley's slowly revolving head calmed him somewhat: he was sure Corley would pull it off all right. All at once the idea struck him that perhaps Corley had seen her home by another way and given him the slip. His eyes searched the street: there was no sign of them. Yet it was surely half-an-hour since he had seen the clock of the College of Surgeons. Would Corley do a thing like that? He lit his last cigarette and began to smoke it nervously. He strained his eyes as each tram stopped at the far corner of the square. They must have gone home by another way. The paper of his cigarette broke and he flung it into the road with a curse.

Suddenly he saw them coming towards him. He started with delight and, keeping close to his lamp-post, tried to read the result in their walk. They were walking quickly, the young woman taking quick short steps, while Corley kept beside her with his long stride. They did not seem to be speaking. An intimation of the result pricked him like the point of a sharp instrument. He knew Corley would fail; he knew it was no go[2].

They turned down Baggot Street and he followed them at once, taking the other footpath. When they stopped he stopped too. They talked for a few moments and then the young woman went down the steps into the area of a house. Corley remained standing at the edge of the path, a little distance from the front steps. Some minutes passed. Then the hall-door was opened slowly

1. College of Surgeons: Stephen's Green West에 있는 The royal College of Surgeons.
2. it's no go: 이젠 다 틀렸다. 가망 없어.(it won't happen.) "no go": useless, futile

and cautiously. A woman came running down the front steps and coughed. Corley turned and went towards her. His broad figure hid hers from view for a few seconds and then she reappeared running up the steps. The door closed on her and Corley began to walk swiftly towards Stephen's Green.

Lenehan hurried on in the same direction. Some drops of light rain fell. He took them as a warning and, glancing back towards the house which the young woman had entered to see that he was not observed, he ran eagerly across the road. Anxiety and his swift run made him pant. He called out:

–Hello, Corley!

Corley turned his head to see who had called him, and then continued walking as before. Lenehan ran after him, settling the waterproof on his shoulders with one hand.

–Hello, Corley! he cried again.

He came level with his friend and looked keenly in his face. He could see nothing there.

Well? he said. Did it come off[3]?

They had reached the corner of Ely Place. Still without answering Corley swerved to the left and went up the side street. His features were composed in stern calm. Lenehan kept up with his friend, breathing uneasily. He was baffled and a note of menace pierced through his voice.

–Can't you tell us? he said. Did you try her?

Corley halted at the first lamp and stared grimly before him. Then with a grave gesture he extended a hand towards the light and, smiling, opened it slowly to the gaze of his disciple. A small gold coin[4] shone in the palm.

---

3. come off: succeed.
4. a small gold coin: 20 실링짜리 금화(a sovereign).

AFTER YOU READ

1. What did Lenehan do until he was included in a round?

2. What released Corley and Lenehan from their silence?

3. How did Lenehan pass the hours till he met Corley again?

4. Corley opened his hand slowly to Lenehan. A small gold coin shone in the palm. What can we infer from the above sentence?

오병석

경희대학교 영어교육과 졸업
경희대학교 영문학 석사
세종대학교 영문학 박사
서일대학 영어과 교수

ENGLISH READING FOR COLLEGE STUDENTS

1판 1쇄 발행 _ 2011년 8월 30일
1판 2쇄 발행 _ 2015년 2월 28일

편 주 자 • 오 병 석
발 행 인 • 정 현 걸
발 행 • 신 아 사
인 쇄 • 예지인쇄
출판등록 • 1956년 1월 5일 (제9-52호)
주 소 • 서울특별시 은평구 녹번동 28-36번지 2층
전 화 • 02)382-6411
팩 스 • 02)382-6401
홈페이지 • www.shinasa.co.kr
E-MAIL • shinasa@chol.com

ISBN 978-89-8396-744-2 (93740)

정가 12,000원